Contents

REPORT DOCUMENTATION PAGE

Form Approved OMB No. 0704-0188

Public reporting burden for this collection of information is estimated to average 1 hour per response, including the time for reviewing instructions, searching existing data sources, gathering and maintaining the data needed, and completing and reviewing this collection of information. Send comments regarding this burden estimate or any other aspect of this collection of information, including suggestions for reducing this burden to Department of Defense, Washington Headquarters Services, Directorate for Information Operations and Reports (0704-0188), 1215 Jefferson Davis Highway, Suite 1204, Arlington, VA 22202-4302. Respondents should be aware that notwithstanding any other provision of law, no person shall be subject to any penalty for failing to comply with a collection of information if it does not display a currently valid OMB control number. PLEASE DO NOT RETURN YOUR FORM TO THE ABOVE ADDRESS.

1. REPORT DATE (DD-MM-YYYY) 01-11-2001	2. REPORT TYPE Handbook	3. DATES COVERED (FROM - TO) xx-xx-2001 to xx-xx-2001

4. TITLE AND SUBTITLE
Commercial Item Handbook (Version 1.0)
Unclassified

5a. CONTRACT NUMBER
5b. GRANT NUMBER
5c. PROGRAM ELEMENT NUMBER

6. AUTHOR(S)

5d. PROJECT NUMBER
5e. TASK NUMBER
5f. WORK UNIT NUMBER

7. PERFORMING ORGANIZATION NAME AND ADDRESS
Office of the Secretary of Defense
Acquisition, Technology, and Logistics
(Acquisition Initiatives)
xxxxx, xxxxxxx

8. PERFORMING ORGANIZATION REPORT NUMBER

9. SPONSORING/MONITORING AGENCY NAME AND ADDRESS
,

10. SPONSOR/MONITOR'S ACRONYM(S)

11. SPONSOR/MONITOR'S REPORT NUMBER(S)

12. DISTRIBUTION/AVAILABILITY STATEMENT
APUBLIC RELEASE

13. SUPPLEMENTARY NOTES

14. ABSTRACT
The purpose of the Handbook is to help acquisition personnel develop sound business strategies for procuring commercial items. The Handbook focuses on how market research and cross-competency teaming can increase the Government?s cost-effective use of commercial items to meet warfighter needs. The Handbook offers suggestions on questions to ask, and it points to additional sources of information, sources of training, and available tools. The Handbook is designed to be a practical reference tool for use in commercial item acquisitions. Appendix B defines terms used in the Handbook.

15. SUBJECT TERMS

16. SECURITY CLASSIFICATION OF:	17. LIMITATION OF ABSTRACT Public Release	18. NUMBER OF PAGES 94	19. NAME OF RESPONSIBLE PERSON Fenster, Lynn lfenster@dtic.mil
a. REPORT Unclassified b. ABSTRACT Unclassified c. THIS PAGE Unclassified			19b. TELEPHONE NUMBER International Area Code Area Code Telephone Number 703767-9007 DSN 427-9007

Standard Form 298 (Rev. 8-98)
Prescribed by ANSI Std Z39.18

Figures

Appendices

Foreword

On January 5, 2001, the Under Secretary of Defense (Acquisition, Technology and Logistics) (USD[AT&L]) issued a policy memorandum to provide immediate clarification on commercial item acquisitions (see Appendix A).This *Commercial Item Handbook* has been issued to provide further guidance on sound business strategies for acquiring commercial items.

PURPOSE

The purpose of the *Handbook* is to help acquisition personnel develop sound business strategies for procuring commercial items. The *Handbook* focuses on how market research and cross-competency teaming can increase the Government's cost-effective use of commercial items to meet warfighter needs. The *Handbook* offers suggestions on questions to ask, and it points to additional sources of information, sources of training, and available tools. The *Handbook* is designed to be a practical reference tool for use in commercial item acquisitions. Appendix B defines terms used in the *Handbook*.

BACKGROUND

Since the passage of the Federal Acquisition Streamlining Act of 1994 (FASA), the preference within the Federal Government has shifted from the acquisition of items developed exclusively for the Government to the acquisition of commercial items. This change was necessary to take full advantage of available and evolving technological innovations in the commercial sector. The Government's increased reliance on commercial items is essential to provide technology solutions that increase warfighter capabilities.

COMMERCIAL ITEM DEFINITION

The definition of "commercial item" is broad. It encompasses items that have been offered for sale to the general public but not yet sold; items that have been sold but not in "substantial" quantities; items requiring modifications customary in the marketplace or minor modifications unique to the Government; many services; and certain nondevelopmental items (see Appendix B, Definitions). This broad definition enables the Government to take greater advantage of the commercial marketplace.

Acquisition professionals must begin each acquisition by conducting market research appropriate to the circumstances to determine if the supply or service to be procured (even if only at a sub-system level) is available commercially. Only after careful review of the commercial item definition—and the gathering of significant evidence that the item is *not* commercial—should they consider the item Government-unique. The following sources are available for exploring the multifaceted "commercial item" definition:

◆ Appendix C, Commercial Item Definition Discussion.

◆ Appendix D, Sample Commercial Item Checklist.

Chapter 1
Describing Agency Needs

Mission need is the preeminent concern in developing requirements documents. The Government has substantial latitude to describe its needs in terms that take optimum advantage of the best industry practices available, such as distribution and support options, methods for assuring reliability, and other capabilities of the marketplace. The essential supply/service characteristics defined during requirements identification should not change in other stages, such as market research and acquisition. However, all members of the acquisition team need to be open to adapting the requirements description and the acquisition strategy as market research permits a greater understanding of how commercial items may be used to satisfy mission needs. Requirements personnel and contracting officers should work together to ensure that commercial items can be—and are—used. The key to this process is aggressive and thorough market research, which is discussed in Chapter 2.

STATING REQUIREMENTS AND DEVELOPING ACQUISITION STRATEGIES

Every acquisition begins with a series of steps addressing important questions such as the following:

◆ What supply/service is required, and how can this requirement be stated in a performance-based manner? (Note that, by statute, when a service is required, performance-based methods are the preferred approach.)

◆ What general capabilities are available in the marketplace to satisfy the requirement?

◆ Can commercial items or modified commercial items satisfy the requirement?

◆ How can the basic requirements statement be refined to maximize the benefit of competitive market forces and the use of commercial items without increasing the potential for product failure and/or greater life cycle costs?

To the utmost extent possible, Government requirements must be stated in terms of measurable standards—functions to be performed, desired performance, or essential physical characteristics. (Whatever way performance standards are described, it is important that they be easily measured using a minimum amount of Government resources.) This mandate promotes the use of a commercial item to fulfill the end-user's needs. A second way of encouraging commercial firms to offer new and innovative products/services to fulfill the end-user's needs is to state requirements in industry-standard terminology and permit the use of commercial practices.

Drafting performance-based requirements begins with the drafting of a statement of the user's need, including a number of performance features the end-user would like to have. This statement should define the operational need for the item, including the intended application, and should also define the desired support services, such as training, testing, maintenance, and repair services. Stating requirements in a performance-based manner, rather than specifying exactly how the item should be manufactured or the service performed, allows for a greater field of offerors and solutions, thereby increasing the possibility that previously unforeseen solutions available in the commercial marketplace will emerge to fulfill the mission requirements.

As the process to refine requirements continues, other factors such as supplier capabilities and logistics support that could impact the requirements should also be considered. Additionally, factors such as product availability and upgrade plans, as well as customary warranty and reliability assurances, should be considered and their impact appropriately discussed in the acquisition planning stage. Budget realities often dictate the need for price-versus-performance tradeoffs, but again, tradeoffs should not fundamentally change the essential performance characteristics. The basis for making these types of decisions and tradeoffs is established through market research.

The clear definition of hardware and software interfaces is another factor to consider in developing requirements and acquisition strategies when several sub-systems will be linked together within a single system. Periodically, software interfaces may need to be redesigned to keep up with evolving commercial technology and improve total weapon system performance. Where appropriate, the Government should develop acquisition strategies that make contractors responsible for managing software interfaces and that encourage the seamless integration of technology upgrades into existing systems. Also, requirements should be written in such a way as to encourage the acquisition of commercial items at the sub-system or component level, where appropriate.

In the requirements and acquisition strategy development process, the Government should not expect or require the contractor to provide detailed design data for commercial items. This strategy can go a long way to remove a barrier identified by contractors reluctant to do business with the Government and can increase access to innovative solutions available as a result of a larger market of opportunity.

PERFORMANCE-BASED REQUIREMENTS DESCRIPTIONS

The key aspects of a performance-based requirements description include

- ◆ a description of the expected output or outcomes or a statement expressing the performance characteristics,

- ◆ a definition of the environment in which the work will be performed,

- ◆ measurement criteria to gauge actual versus expected performance, and

- ◆ procedures for re-performance or reduction in price if the item or service does not meet the performance standards.

Requirements descriptions that have these characteristics are called performance-based statements of work, or statements of objectives. A well-thought-out performance-based requirements description is essential for ensuring that the Government receives a supply or service that meets the established requirements. Performance-based requirements descriptions state the Government's required outcomes and provide criteria for measuring and verifying performance; they do not dictate the specific methods to be used to achieve those outcomes. It is essential to perform a thorough job analysis so that appropriate, measurable performance standards (outputs) including appropriate quality levels can be set forth in the solicitation. Tying contractor compensation and financial risk to successful achievement of these quality and performance standards increases the chances that the Government will receive supplies or services that fulfill its requirements. For resources related to performance-based requirements descriptions, see Appendix E.

Chapter 2
Market Research

Although acquisition personnel have historically engaged in market research, in today's environment, to ensure that high-quality Defense solutions are provided to the end-user at a reasonable price, it is necessary to conduct that research in greater depth. Further, it is essential that today's market research be conducted by drawing on the knowledge of all team members up front, to ensure ongoing access to evolving technologies. Additionally, acquisition personnel must create acquisition strategies that facilitate the introduction or incorporation of evolving commercial items into Defense systems.

When market research indicates that the Government's need can be met by an item of supply or a service that meets the broad definition of a commercial item and that is of a type customarily available in the marketplace, then the contracting officer *must* solicit and award a contract using the commercial item acquisition policies found in Federal Acquisition Regulation (FAR) Part 12. If market research indicates that commercial items might not be available to satisfy the agency's needs, the agency must reevaluate those needs and determine whether they can be restated so as to permit the use of commercial items.

When thorough market research indicates that commercial items are not available to meet the Government's needs, the contracting officer must include Numbered Note 26 in the presolicitation synopsis. This note notifies potential offerors that interested persons have 15 days to indicate their ability to satisfy the requirement with a commercial item. Any "commercial" item identified by a potential offeror in response to Numbered Note 26 must be evaluated for technical acceptability.

Figure 1 depicts how market research drives much of the preaward process.

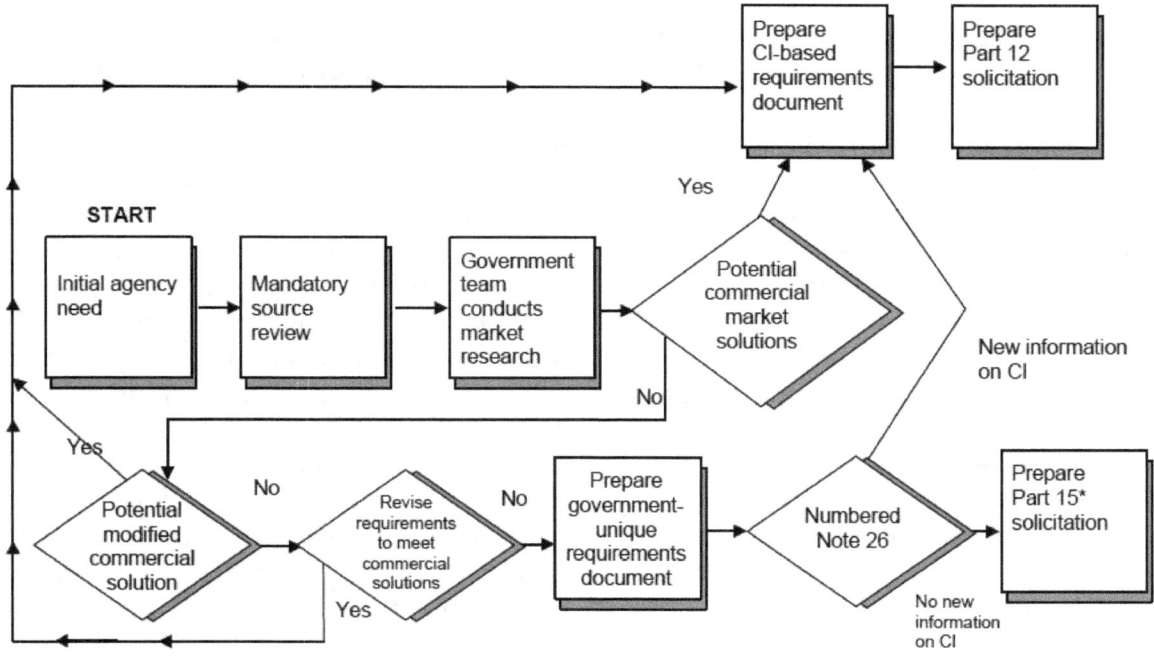

Figure 1. Market Research Drives the Preaward Process

CI = Commercial item
*Even though Part 14 is available for use, it does not match well with FAR Part 12.
FAR Part 14 is designed for procurements with highly specific statements of work.
FAR Part 12 often relies on performance specifications.

SIGNIFICANCE OF MARKET RESEARCH

DoD conducts market research to arrive at the most suitable approach to acquiring, distributing, and supporting supplies and services and to determine potential sources. Some specific benefits that may accrue from performing thorough market research include:

◆ minimizing the risk of doing business, for both the Government and the contractor;

◆ uncovering and identifying potential problems, thereby reducing risks associated with contingencies;

◆ obtaining information to support price reasonableness determinations;

◆ creating a benchmark to track progress during contract performance;

◆ evaluating the contract's success;

◆ identifying additional sources; and

◆ understanding better the options available to satisfy the Government's requirement.

Team-Driven

Broadly speaking, the Government uses market research to collect information in three areas: technical, pricing, and terms and conditions. DoD does not have a specific job category called "market researcher"; instead, a wide range of professionals are called upon to perform market research related to their area of expertise. Traditionally, the program management office or the requiring activity has conducted the market research, relying heavily on inputs almost entirely from the technical community. However, in this new business environment, representatives from all disciplines (e.g., technical, contracting, logistics, and costing) need to be included early in the process. (For a discussion of the composition of the market research team, see Appendix F.) Information gathered during market research should be used to refine the requirements so as to maximize the benefit of competitive market forces. To provide input to the team on acquisition strategy, procurement/contracting personnel gather information on customary contract terms and conditions for acquiring the type of item or service being procured, representative incentive provisions, customary practices of the particular industry regarding product modifications and tailoring, and expected pricing practices. To provide input to the team on product life-cycle decisions, logistics personnel need insight into standard industry practices regarding reliability incentives versus warranties, product obsolescence, and spares provisions. To obtain the greatest benefit from using commercial practices, it is necessary to consider all aspects of the business strategy up front.

In the absence of specific agency guidance or individual team arrangement, the contracting officer should take the responsibility for the market research effort. A partnership between contracting and requirements personnel is especially crucial to the market research effort. Contracting personnel need the input, guidance, and support of requirements personnel to enable the use of commercial item acquisitions by identifying possible commercial components and technologies. Contracting personnel need to be actively engaged as part of the market research effort to help all members of the acquisition team find satisfactory solutions that both stay within the bounds of regulations and preserve the integrity of the acquisition process. (For example, requirements personnel play a vital role early in the market research process but a background role in later processes such as negotiations, evaluation, and source selection.)

Continuous Activity

It is important that market research continue throughout an acquisition, in order to gather the kind of data needed for making smart acquisition decisions. Information is a changing commodity, and sound business judgments depend on up-to-date details. The team actively conducts market research to develop a sound acquisition strategy, a good understanding of customary commercial terms and conditions, and sufficient information to enable the achievement of fair and reasonable pricing. The level of detail gathered may vary by stage in the acquisition process. When the initial requirements statement is being developed, a general understanding of terms and conditions and pricing may suffice for making higher-level requirements analysis judgments. However, to be sure that the market will be able to respond to the Government's needs, and to ensure that the final acquisition strategy and the solicitation will fit the particular market's customary business practices, a more in-depth understanding of the types of terms and conditions being offered commercially will be required. Furthermore, firm knowledge of market pricing information is necessary for planning for contract obligations and determining price reasonableness. As the acquisition matures, the market research information will need to be increasingly precise.

Appropriate to the Circumstances

Since market research is a business operation, it should be conducted in a cost-effective manner. This means that its extent will vary, depending on such factors as urgency, estimated dollar value, complexity, and past experience. It will be necessary to conduct market research appropriate to the circumstances before developing new requirements documents and before soliciting above the simplified acquisition threshold.

MARKET RESEARCH TECHNIQUES

Some market research techniques include

- ◆ contacting knowledgeable individuals in Government and industry regarding market capabilities,

- ◆ reviewing results of recent market research reports covering similar items,

- ◆ publishing formal requests for information,

- ◆ querying Internet information sources,

- ◆ obtaining source lists from other agencies or from associations,

- ◆ reviewing catalogs and product literature, and

- ◆ conducting interchange meetings or holding presolicitation conferences and other Government-industry interchanges.

THE MARKET RESEARCH REPORT

Not only the current acquisition, but future commercial item acquisitions can benefit from the teaming and market research involved in any given commercial item acquisition—but only if a market research report is produced to capture for future application the details of that acquisition. The Government should document and retain for future reference potentially useful aspects of market research, in a manner appropriate to the size and complexity of the acquisition. Appendix G sets forth a sample market research report format; however, individual judgment ought to be used in each acquisition to determine just which details are important for inclusion in the final report. Many appendices in this handbook provide useful market research information, including Appendix D, Sample Commercial Item Checklist; Appendix G, Sample Market Research Report; Appendix H, Market Research Questions—Historical Acquisition Information; Appendix I, Market Research Resources; Appendix L, Market Research—Pricing Information Sources;

Appendix M, Market Research Questions—Price-Related Information; and Appendix N, Price Analysis Techniques.

MARKET RESEARCH PRICING CONSIDERATIONS

Market research must be used when developing Government requirements and determining how to satisfy them. This research is required because the decisions made in the presolicitation phase will be key factors in defining what the Government receives and the price the Government will pay. Better understanding of the marketplace increases the likelihood that the Government's needs will be met at a reasonable price.

This same understanding of the marketplace will provide the basis for developing more accurate contract price estimates than have historically been available. Preliminary price estimates resulting from thorough market research, as well as increased insight into the factors that affect contract price, will be key inputs to the acquisition planning process and possibly even to the final determination of price reasonableness. Chapter 4 provides more detail on the importance of market research with regard to pricing commercial items.

USING ACQUISITION HISTORY TO SUPPORT MARKET RESEARCH

Contracting officers should review the acquisition history of the supplies or services. This review helps ensure that all relevant prior prices are considered in estimating the proper price of the current acquisition. Part of that price relevancy review should include an assessment of any historical documentation related to the prior price reasonableness determination.

HISTORICAL ACQUISITION INFORMATION AND QUESTIONS

Historical data provide a picture of what happened in the past. It is important to give appropriate consideration to how changes might have affected the current acquisition environment. The table presented in Appendix H highlights questions the Government should consider when market research is completed.

MARKET RESEARCH RESOURCES

See Appendix I for sources that can be consulted when performing market research.

Chapter 3
Acquiring Commercial Items

COMMERCIAL ITEM DEFINITION

The commercial item definition (see Appendixes B and C) is broad. It embraces any item of a type customarily used by the general public or by nongovernmental entities for purposes other than Government purposes that has been sold, leased, or licensed or offered for sale, lease, or license to the general public. Also included in the commercial item definition is any item that has evolved from a commercial item as described above, through technical/performance advances, even if it is not yet available in the commercial marketplace, as long as it will be available in time to satisfy the Government's requirements. Commercial items do not necessarily have to be "off-the-shelf"; items that merely require modifications of a type customarily available in the commercial marketplace, or else minor Government-unique modifications, can still be considered commercial items. (To qualify as representing a minor modification, the item must retain a predominance of nongovernmental functions or physical characteristics.) Additionally, the FAR commercial item definition includes many services. A service is considered a commercial item when it is provided in support of a commercial item as previously defined. A service is also considered a commercial item when it is of a type offered and sold competitively in substantial quantities in the commercial market on the basis of established catalog or market prices for specific tasks performed under standard commercial terms and conditions. The definition also includes any combination of commercial items (except "of a type" services) that are customarily combined and sold in combination to the general public.

The commercial item definition is not limited to items acquired by the Government from prime contractors; it also extends to commercial items acquired from subcontractors at all tiers, including items transferred from a contractor's divisions, affiliates, or subsidiaries. Acquisition professionals are responsible for developing requirements and acquisition strategies that facilitate the inclusion of commercial items in Government-unique systems.

Commercial off-the-shelf (COTS) items, nondevelopmental items (NDIs), and Government off-the-shelf (GOTS) items are related to commercial items, but the terms are not synonymous. Further, the fact that a supply or service to be procured does not easily fit into the NDI or GOTS categories does not in itself mean that it is not a commercial item. (For more details, see Appendix J.)

COMMON MISPERCEPTIONS ABOUT COMMERCIAL ITEM ACQUISITIONS

Some members of the acquisition community have expressed concern that FAR Part 12 contracts afford the Government less assurance that the acquisition will result in receipt of a high-quality product. But a well-planned and well-constructed commercial acquisition can provide greater protection against poor quality than a Government-unique contract provides. When a commercial market exists for a product, the Government should be able to choose from a range of supplies or services providing the best value to the Government.

Additionally, a product does not have to be developed at private expense to be commercial. Even if the Government has paid for its development, or even if it has a military origin, a commercial market might subsequently develop for it. The issue of who paid for development is not part of the commercial item determination. Furthermore, the offered price is not part of the commercial item determination. The commerciality determination precedes and is separate from the price reasonableness determination.

Along these same lines, the fact that an item may meet unique Government requirements does not, in and of itself, mean that it is a Government-unique item. Other misperceptions about commercial items include the inaccurate beliefs that the exact part number must be sold in the commercial market, a commercial service cannot be performed on a military item, and a commercial item cannot be incorporated into a military system.

An item is commercial because of the supply or service itself, not because of who provides the item. For example, a Government source such as NIB/NISH can be governed by a FAR Part 12 contract for janitorial services even if it does not provide those services in a commercial market.

MAKING COMMERCIAL ITEM DETERMINATIONS

Because they rely on flexibility and the exercise of sound business judgment by Government acquisition personnel, commercial item policies and procedures also rely heavily on the education, training, and professional expertise of acquisition personnel. An inevitable by-product of the reliance on business judgment is wide variation in interpretations and application of policies and procedures. The decision as to whether the Government's requirements for a specific acquisition can be met by a commercial item is based on market research and an analysis of the marketplace.

Several alternative approaches can be used to streamline the item-by-item determination process currently in use. See Appendix K for a discussion of these alternative approaches, which are intended to increase the consistency of decisions across a department or agency.

SUBCONTRACT COMMERCIAL ITEM DETERMINATION

All requirements should be drafted to require that both the prime contractors and subcontractors at all levels incorporate commercial items, to the maximum extent practicable, as components of items supplied to the agency. The prime contractor has the authority and responsibility for determining whether an item to be supplied by a subcontractor is a commercial item. Contractors and subcontractors at all tiers are expected to exercise reasonable business judgment in making such determinations, as with any other subcontracting-related decision. All commercial item decisions are expected to be consistent with the guidelines set forth in the FAR.

Chapter 4
Pricing Commercial Items

In the commercial marketplace, knowing what is being bought and assessing the relative value of an item from the customer's perspective are more important than knowing the cost incurred by the supplier. When people buy a television set, they don't review the cost of the components, materials, transportation, and so forth. Instead, they consider product features, the reputation of manufacturers (i.e., previous performance), relative prices of various brands and models, and the like and make a best-value selection consistent with their personal needs and budget constraints. The amount of profit the manufacturer makes is irrelevant, as long as the customer believes that the product received represents the best value available from the alternatives considered. Likewise, when commercial items are bought for the Government, the emphasis is on market research and on obtaining the best value, taking into account not only price but also quality considerations.

MARKET RESEARCH

Market research can be used to locate many sources of pricing information, including those identified in Appendix L. Thorough market research will help to identify market conditions or other factors that may affect the price of the item or service. The determination of price reasonableness can be based upon the following items or combination of items:

- ◆ Prices for commercial items sold, or offered for sale, to the public.

- ◆ Potential value of modifications to commercial items.

- ◆ Acquisition histories, including prices paid for purchases of similar items.

- ◆ Prices for similar items on mandatory and optional schedules.

- ◆ Product catalogs and price lists.

For the final two items above, the contracting officer should also determine what prices were actually paid, rather than just relying on the published schedule, catalog, or price list. Suppliers often discount published prices, and a price reasonableness determination should take such price reductions into account.

Pricing Factors

The table in Appendix M identifies the type of price-related questions that the Government should be able to answer when market research is completed.

Market Leverage—The Key to Reasonable Prices and Best Value

A thorough understanding of the marketplace is necessary for adequately evaluating factors that influence pricing in a particular market. Each marketplace has its unique characteristics and dynamics; therefore, buyers and sellers enter the marketplace with different amounts of leverage. Leverage is determined by a number of factors in addition to the traditional forces of supply and demand that make buyers and sellers attractive business partners to one another. Buyers increase their leverage when larger quantities are purchased, full lines of products and services offered are taken advantage of, flexible terms and conditions are used, unique requirements or specifications are minimized, long-term partnerships are committed to, existing commercial distribution systems are used, and so forth. The more attractive the Government can make itself as a buyer, the more likely it is that world-class sellers will enter into contracts with the Government, that favorable terms and conditions will be negotiated, and that lower prices will be paid.

By understanding the requirement as well as the marketplace, the acquisition team is better able to match marketplace capability with customer need. Every member of the acquisition team has a role in ensuring that the Government has maximum leverage in the marketplace. By working as a team, the various functional experts can achieve optimum results instead of simply maximizing the outcome according to the narrow perspective of the expert's particular functional area. The grouping and timing of requirements, the specifications and packaging, testing requirements, payment terms, and the like can all influence the ability to get the best deal for the Government. Often, trade-offs among the various functional experts on the team are necessary.

PRICE ANALYSIS

Commercial items—like any other supplies or services bought by the Government—must be purchased at fair and reasonable prices. Price analysis, supported by market research, is the preferred method for determining whether prices paid for commercial items are fair and reasonable. (See Appendix B for a definition of price analysis.) Price analysis techniques include those identified in Appendix N.

Appropriate Level of Effort

The level of effort expended to determine price reasonableness should be commensurate with the circumstances of the acquisition. The total dollar value of the procurement and the urgency of the requirement are two factors to consider when making that determination. For example, it would be inappropriate to unreasonably delay an award for repair parts for a piece of equipment if greater costs are being incurred because the equipment is out of service. Likewise, it would not be appropriate to incur reverse engineering expenses unless it is likely that savings on future procurements will offset the cost of doing so. In any event, the level of effort expended should enable a determination that a price is fair and reasonable.

Negotiating Fair and Reasonable Prices

The fact that a published price exists for a commercial item under consideration does not necessarily mean that the price is fair and reasonable. Developing an effective bargaining position is important in any acquisition. Armed with the results of their market research and other information, buyers should be able and willing to challenge offered prices—especially those that appear unreasonable.

Both the buyer and the seller have an equal right to engage in hard bargaining. At the same time, the ultimate success of acquisition reinvention depends upon two-way cooperation and a desire by both parties to establish and maintain a mutually advantageous business relationship. If a seller is unwilling to negotiate, this behavior should be documented as part of historical acquisition data and considered in future source selections.

Reverse Auctioning

Reverse auctioning over the Internet can be used as a pricing tool to obtain the information necessary to render a best-value determination. It can also be used to bring competition to a Government supply list. Reverse auctions are marketplaces in which many sellers compete for the buyer's purchase. A buyer issues a request for supplies or services, and sellers respond in real time with their offers. Where competition exists, the reverse auction environment results in driving down the sellers' offered prices. Several online sources for reverse auctioning exist, including the General Services Administration's (GSA's) Buyers.gov (http://www.buyers.gov), which marries the Federal Supply Schedules (FSS) and reverse auctioning.

Cost Accounting Standards

The applicability of Cost Accounting Standards (CAS) is an important consideration in pricing many acquisitions. However, by law, CAS rules do not apply to contracts and subcontracts for the acquisition of commercial items.

SOLE-SOURCE SITUATIONS

Contracting officers and requirements personnel should work together to avoid sole-source situations. Competition is enabled when needs are broadly stated in terms of performance outcomes. However, a sole-source situation may be unavoidable, presenting pricing challenges. Commercial buyers can pay "whatever the market will bear" to get a needed part, although smart buying practices include obtaining reasonable prices. Government buyers procuring the same items are still held to the higher standard of "fair and reasonable." The procedures and techniques set forth above for market research and price analysis will provide the best opportunity to acquire items at reasonable prices. Opportunities to obtain any form of market leverage in these situations may be limited. However, Appendix O illustrates how some techniques may be useful in achieving fair and reasonable prices even when the Government has a minimum of market leverage.

Need for Additional Data to Determine the Price To Be Fair and Reasonable

If, after market research has been conducted and the appropriate price analysis techniques have been applied, the offeror's price for a sole-source commercial item cannot be determined to be fair and reasonable, then the contracting officer may require the offeror to submit cost information to support further analysis. Contracting officers should not require more data than necessary to make the price reasonableness determination. Contracting officers may not require contractors to certify any supporting cost information.

Even with the aid of uncertified cost information, a contracting officer may be unable to conclude that the price a sole-source supplier asks is fair and reasonable. (This also could be true even in traditional procurements using certified cost or pricing data and cost analysis.) When the contracting officer cannot conclude that the price of a commercial item is fair and reasonable, after exploring the various market alternatives that would effectively meet the agency's needs with the requiring activity and other members of the acquisition team, the contracting officer should consider any suitable noncommercial items. If there are none, the contracting officer should escalate negotiations in accordance with agency procedures. If the price still cannot be determined to be fair and reasonable, the item ordinarily should not be acquired. If, however, it is not in the Government's best interest to forgo or delay the procurement, then it is essential that the contracting officer document the difficulty he or she had in determining the price to be fair and reasonable. The contracting officer then may make the award. Careful file documentation will enable subsequent buyers to fully understand the circumstances surrounding the prices paid, should there be a need for future acquisitions of the same item. If the requirement is likely to recur, it is imperative that the acquisition team take any steps necessary to enhance the Government's market leverage and negotiating position prior to the next procurement.

INNOVATION AND INCENTIVES

Contracting officers can also use innovative acquisition strategies and pricing incentives to encourage fair pricing and favorable business practices. Favorable outcomes can also be considered, such as cost reductions to the Government resulting from improved support services. Enhanced performance levels can also be rewarded through the Government's evaluation criteria. For instance, the Government can provide a higher evaluation rating to a company that has demonstrated a positive reliability curve for its supplies.

The Department of the Navy has developed a Naval Strategy for Commercial Contracting. In a memorandum dated April 24, 2000, Navy buyers are encouraged to incorporate an innovative commercial contracting strategy using a two-phased approach involving a commercial area announcement followed by a request for commercial offering. For additional innovative acquisition strategies, see the Army's report entitled *Constructing Successful Business Relationships: Innovation in Contractual Incentives*, or the Air Force's *Award Fee and Award Term Guide*. The Army's report suggests award term contracting as a successful strategy. Under award term contracting, the Government establishes objective performance parameters in the underlying contract and announces up front that it intends to shorten or lengthen the period of performance (minimum and maximum) on the basis of the contractor's performance against those parameters.

CONFIGURATION CONTROL AND LOGISTICS SUPPORT

An important aspect of pricing is the consideration of life-cycle costs, including configuration control and logistics support. Systems managers need to design and plan for the appropriate level of configuration control, one that is tied to the long-term support strategy (e.g., contractor support versus organic support, and at what levels). For more details on this topic, see Appendix P.

PRICING SUPPORT RESOURCES

The sources listed in Appendix Q are available to provide pricing support.

Chapter 5
Contracting for Commercial Items

CONTRACT TYPE

To the maximum extent practicable, agencies must use firm-fixed-price contracts or fixed-price contracts with economic price adjustment for the acquisition of commercial items. These contract types may be used in conjunction with an award-fee incentive and performance or delivery incentives when the award fee or incentive is based solely on factors other than cost. Indefinite-delivery contracts, including single- or multiple-award task order contracts or delivery order contracts and the Federal Supply Schedules, may be used when the prices are established on the basis of a firm fixed price or a fixed price with economic price adjustment. Use of cost-reimbursement contracts to acquire commercial items is prohibited.

For services that are available on a time-and-material or labor-hour basis in the commercial market, certain pricing strategies can be used to acquire them through Part 12, as long as the contract type itself remains within the parameters discussed above. One strategy is the use of an indefinite-delivery contract with established fixed hourly rates that permit negotiating orders (including any required materials). A second strategy is the use of sequential contract actions that acquire the requirement in modular components. An example of this strategy is a preliminary firm-fixed-price "diagnostic" effort allowing the contractor to understand the scope of the work sufficiently to propose the larger requirement on a firm-fixed-price basis.

CONTRACTING POLICIES AND PROCEDURES

The question arises often of how the policies for acquiring commercial items fit with the other acquisition policies and procedures. FAR Part 12 prescribes policies and procedures unique to the acquisition of commercial items, but it is not a "stand alone" part. The FAR Part 12 policies must be used in conjunction with the policies and procedures for solicitation, evaluation, and award of contracts and orders set forth in either Part 13, Simplified Acquisition Procedures; Part 14, Sealed Bidding; or Part 15, Contracting by Negotiation, as appropriate for the particular acquisition.

FAR Subpart 13.5 authorizes a test program that allows issuance of solicitations under simplified acquisition procedures for procuring supplies and services in amounts greater than the simplified acquisition threshold but not exceeding $5 million, including options. Currently this authority will expire on January 1, 2002. The test program allows FAR Part 13 procedures to be used if the contracting officer reasonably expects—on the basis of the nature of the supplies or services sought and market research—that offers will include only commercial items. Under this test program, contracting officers may use any simplified acquisition procedure in FAR Part 13, subject to the specific dollar limitation applicable to that particular procedure. The test program's purpose is to vest contracting officers with additional procedural discretion and flexibility, so that commercial item acquisitions in this dollar range may be solicited, offered, evaluated, and awarded in a simplified manner that maximizes efficiency and economy and minimizes the burden and administrative costs for both the Government and industry.

COMMERCIAL ITEM TERMS AND CONDITIONS

Contracts for procuring commercial items must, to the maximum extent practicable, include only those contract clauses needed to implement law, regulation, or Executive Order or determined to be consistent with customary commercial practice. To implement this mandate, FAR Part 12 prescribes limited solicitation provisions and contract clauses. They are a compilation of the FAR provisions and clauses considered most likely to apply to commercial items. (See Appendix R for further details.)

FAR Part 12 minimizes the number of provisions and clauses required for commercial item acquisitions. Notwithstanding prescriptions contained elsewhere in the FAR, when acquiring commercial items, contracting officers need use only those provisions and clauses prescribed in Part 12. Note, however, that since the FAR Part 12 provisions and clauses were written to address commercial market practices covering a wide range of potential commercial item acquisitions, they usually need to be tailored to suit the specific acquisition. The bottom line is that, instead of requiring contracting officers to include standard FAR provisions and clauses in accordance with their prescriptions, FAR Part 12 provides significantly increased flexibility to negotiate a mutually satisfactory agreement.

While the Part 12 provisions and clauses will suffice for a wide range commercial item acquisitions, it sometimes may be appropriate to incorporate provisions or clauses from elsewhere in the FAR to protect the Government's interest. Accordingly, contracting officers need to exercise good business judgment and consider policies and terms and conditions in other parts of the FAR that may be appropriate for assuring the successful performance of a proposed acquisition. Note, however, that other FAR provisions and clauses can be used only when their use is consistent with customary commercial practices or when a waiver is obtained in accordance with agency procedures. The customary terms and conditions will vary depending on the product (e.g., customary terms for launch services will not be the same as those for standard software). The incorporation of such terms and conditions will typically result in tailoring solicitation provisions and clauses, discussed in the following section.

TAILORING PROVISIONS AND CLAUSES

Within certain limits, the contracting officer can tailor the FAR Part 12 commercial item provisions and clauses to adapt to the particular commercial market in which he or she is working. The FAR gives contracting officers authority to tailor solicitation provisions and contract clauses when the tailoring is consistent with commercial practices for the item being procured. Tailoring in a manner inconsistent with commercial practice requires approval in accordance with agency procedures. For more details on tailoring, see Appendix R.

Government procurement professionals are responsible for conducting market research in order to be familiar with the details of commercial buying and selling practices. Be aware that, in the commercial marketplace, both "seller's" and "buyer's" terms exist; know which version is being proffered as "standard commercial practice." A "customary" practice does not have to be used by a majority of buyers and sellers, as long as it has been accepted on a regular basis by at least some of the trading partners in that market.

SUBCONTRACTING FOR COMMERCIAL ITEMS

To extend the benefits of commercial item acquisitions to the subcontractor level, contracts set forth limitations on the applicability of certain laws and contract clauses to the acquisition of commercial items at the subcontractor level. In some cases, use of commercial items on the subcontract level is more viable than their use on prime contracts. For further details on this matter, see Appendix R.

Chapter 6
Administering Commercial Item Contracts

The Government performs contract administration to ensure that the contractor meets its contractual obligations so that the end-user obtains necessary and suitable goods and services at the time they are needed. Some of the functions performed in the contract administration phase include technical surveillance, inspection and acceptance, change order and claim administration, and financial and negotiation services. Contract administration functions do not include making commerciality determinations for subcontracts, since such decisions are the responsibility of the prime contractor, as discussed in Chapter 3.

Contract administration practices vary considerably between commercial and Government acquisitions, so the contract administration duties as identified in FAR Part 42 generally do not apply to contracts for commercial items. However, some fashion of contract administration is still needed. Contracting officers may negotiate agreements with the appropriate contract administration office covering the delegation of certain functions normally associated with FAR Part 42, but should only include those functions that are appropriate for the commercial item being sold. Agreements documenting the delegation of authority to the Defense Contract Management Agency should clearly state the ways in which commercial practices will affect the administration mechanisms and procedures that historically have been used. Contracting officers should ensure that the functions identified in the delegations are consistent with industry practices.

DoD should focus on value-added contract administration activities in order to streamline its contract administration and audit services, realize cost reductions—for both the Department and its contractors—and further the aims of civil/military integration.

INSPECTION AND ACCEPTANCE

To the maximum extent practicable, the Government must rely on commercial item contractors' existing quality assurance systems as a substitute for Government inspection and testing before tender for acceptance, unless customary commercial market practice for the item being acquired includes buyer-conducted in-process inspection. This implements the FASA preference for reliance on the contractor's existing quality assurance system, which is intended to relieve contractors from having to comply with unnecessary Government-unique testing and inspection.

PERFORMANCE MANAGEMENT

Performance management is a critical element of successful performance-based services acquisitions, including those for commercial items. Performance-based approaches rely upon industry for quality assurance and control. Performance-based approaches also provide incentives as motivation, with the Government periodically assessing performance. To foster successful performance management and improve process capability, DoD and industry should jointly use tools for continuous improvement and process redesign (e.g., internal measurement systems, customer and supplier input, training).

The key to performance management is developing an acquisition strategy that mitigates risk and states contract requirements in performance terms. The performance assessment plan should outline the roles and responsibilities of the parties involved to guarantee that service delivery proceeds in accordance with the performance standards designated in the performance-based statement of work. In effect, the performance assessment plan is a roadmap to ensure that the Government receives high-quality services as specified in the contract, pays only for services rendered at or above the acceptable level, and motivates contractors to attain those levels. A well-developed performance assessment plan also includes an assessment schedule and the assessment methods to be used, along with a description of the actions to be taken if performance standards are not met. This is consistent with the transition from oversight to insight, since it focuses contract administration resources on contractor processes that influence contract performance.

Plans should also address performance assessment and allocate agency resources to monitoring the essential aspects of service delivery. Because contractor remuneration is tied to performance, it is crucial to take considerable care in developing the performance assessment plan. Important elements to consider include (but are not limited to) task criticality, performance requirements and standards, assessment methods, and availability and appropriateness of personnel assigned to carry out performance assessment. Resource constraints are such that assessment activities need to be commensurate with cost and risk.

Common assessment methods (which should be identified in the performance assessment plan) include commercial quality methods (e.g., contract metrics), sampling, and customer surveys. Surveys are useful performance measurement tools because they can provide a balanced means for assessing stakeholder views. The four primary groups to survey are customers, suppliers, employees, and managers. To achieve balance, the survey elicits the stakeholders' opinions on the parameters of service delivery, including quality, timeliness, and efficiency. The customer should use the survey's results in the feedback process to ensure that the service provider's performance is satisfactory—or, if necessary, improves—before milestone payments are made. (Note that the same concept applies to supplies. That is, a performance assessment plan is also necessary for performance-based supplies acquisitions. In the case of an item of supply that is a commercial item, the performance assessment plan may be very short and only establish times for evaluation upon delivery and before payment.)

The service provider may also be involved in developing and implementing the performance assessment process. As a stakeholder whose pay is tied to acceptable performance, the contractor needs to understand, accept, and agree to the terms of the assessment. Obtaining contractor participation early in the process ensures that the contractor's own quality assurance and control plan dovetails with the Government's.

DoD's Guidebook for Performance-Based Services Acquisition (PBSA) includes details of contractor performance management.

Chapter 7
Special Considerations

As has been noted, contracts for acquiring commercial items are subject not only to the policies of FAR Part 12, but also to other parts of the FAR (however, when a conflict between parts exists, FAR Part 12 policy governs). This chapter highlights several of the special considerations that commonly arise—such as those involving the use of Government supply sources (addressed in FAR Part 8) and 8(a) contractors (addressed in FAR Part 19).

GOVERNMENT SUPPLY SOURCES

A variety of Government supply sources are available to satisfy the Government's needs, including those for commercial items. Some supply sources are available on a non-mandatory basis, such as the Federal Supply Schedules—also known as the multiple-award schedules (MAS), Government-wide acquisition contracts (GWACs), and multi-agency contracts. The use of certain other supply sources is mandatory, such as Federal Prison Industries, Inc. (FPI or UNICOR) and nonprofit agencies operating pursuant to the Javits-Wagner-O'Day (JWOD) Act employing people who are blind or severely disabled.

FAR Part 8 addresses use of these sources (with the exception of GWACs and multi-agency contracts). The application of Part 12 varies, depending upon the source from which the purchase is to be made. As described below, commercial item policies and procedures apply to the acquisition of commercial items through MAS, GWACs, and multi-agency contracts. They do not apply to acquisitions from FPI. Application to JWOD purchases is at the discretion of the contracting activity.

Multiple-Award Schedules, Multiple-Award Task and Delivery Order Contracts, Government-Wide Acquisition Contracts, and Multi-Agency Contracts

The General Services Administration (GSA) and the Veterans Administration (VA)—which manages certain schedules for medical supplies pursuant to a delegation from GSA—have designed the MAS program so that purchases for commercial items made under it comport with the commercial item policies of FAR Part 12. FAR Subpart 8.4 addresses purchases through the MAS. The MAS are a non-mandatory priority source for consideration in conducting acquisitions.

Users of GWACs and multi-agency contract vehicles should expect to follow Part 12 when buying commercial items. GWACs and multi-agency contracts are typically structured as multiple-award task and delivery order contracts, whose use is addressed in FAR Subpart 16.5. Contracts established pursuant to FAR Subpart 16.5 are required to be consistent with the policies of Part 12 where acquisitions of commercial items are involved.

Order placement under multiple-award task and delivery order contracts, GWACs, and multi-agency contracts is covered in FAR Subpart 16.5. GWACs and multi-agency contracts, while not addressed in FAR Part 8, are generally designed (like those used with other Government supply sources) to provide broad agency access to goods and services.

For additional discussion regarding use of the MAS and multiple-award task and delivery order contracts (including GWACs and multi-agency contracts) for the acquisition of commercial items, see Appendix S.

Federal Prison Industries, Inc., Program

Commercial item acquisition policies and procedures do not apply to acquisitions from FPI (UNICOR), which is a wholly owned Government corporation. FPI acquisitions still take precedence for listed items and services in the order of priority for required sources of supplies and services and are conducted in accordance with FAR Subpart 8.6.

Javits-Wagner-O'Day Program

While JWOD-participating nonprofit agencies are not commercial entities, the supplies and services they provide are most often commercial. As such, they may be acquired using the commercial item acquisition policies and provisions. The decision whether to conduct JWOD acquisitions using commercial item acquisition policies and procedures can be based on cost-effectiveness, such as automated systems capabilities or other administrative considerations. Regardless of whether commercial item acquisition policies and procedures are used, JWOD Procurement List items are required sources of supplies and services and are conducted in accordance with FAR Subpart 8.7.

Section 8(a) Program

The Section 8(a) Program rules apply to acquisitions of commercial items, whether the contract is placed with the Small Business Administration or directly with the 8(a) contractor (see FAR Subpart 19.8). If commercial items will be procured under the 8(a) Program, FAR Part 12 terms and conditions apply.

Simplified Acquisitions

The question of how the policies for acquiring commercial items fit with the other acquisition policies comes up often, particularly with regard to the use of simplified acquisition procedures. When acquiring any commercial item, contracting officers use not only FAR Part 12, but also the existing FAR procedures in Part 13, 14, or 15. These procedures include oral solicitations, requests for quotations, purchase orders, invitations for bids, and requests for proposals, as appropriate, but the terms and conditions should be tailored to reflect the policies governing the acquisition of commercial items. The Government purchase card is appropriate for most simplified acquisitions less than or equal to the micropurchase threshold; however, when a purchase order or blanket purchase agreement is awarded, use commercial item policies and procedures.

Appendix A
Commercial Acquisitions Policy Memorandum

THE UNDER SECRETARY OF DEFENSE

3010 DEFENSE PENTAGON
WASHINGTON. DC 20301-3010

JAN 5 2001

ACQUISITION AND
TECHNOLOGY

MEMORANDUM FOR SECRETARIES OF THE MILITARY DEPARTMENTS
DIRECTOR, DEFENSE CONTRACT MANAGEMENT AGENCY
DIRECTOR, DEFENSE LOGISTICS AGENCY

SUBJECT: Commercial Acquisitions

Defense acquisitions should emphasize performance-based requirements, include provisions that enable commercial practices, and encourage the participation of nontraditional commercial entities. The efforts of all members of the acquisition team are crucial to achieving increased use of commercial acquisitions, but the input of requirements personnel and program managers is particularly essential, since they impart knowledge of available technology to the team. To the maximum extent possible, commercial acquisitions should be conducted using Federal Acquisition Regulation (FAR) Part 12. The use of FAR Part 12 is designed to provide the Department of Defense (DoD) with greater access to commercial markets with increased competition, better prices, and new market entrants and/or technologies.

In March 1999, I directed the Deputy Under Secretary of Defense (Acquisition Reform) (DUSD (AR)) and the Director of Defense Procurement to charter an Integrated Process Team (IPT) to review DoD commercial item determinations and evaluate whether additional guidance, tools, or training were necessary. The IPT found that, while some progress has been made, many obstacles to accessing commercial items remain. These obstacles include inconsistent commercial item determinations, weak market research, and confusion concerning pricing of commercial items. Additionally, lessons learned as to the applicability of FAR Part 12 determinations are not being shared across DoD buying offices. These factors unnecessarily increase workload and acquisition cycle time.

To help overcome these barriers to accessing commercial items, I am taking the following actions:

- ◆ Providing clarification on FAR Part 12 use to yield appropriate consistency across DoD;
- ◆ Establishing goals that DUSD(AR) will track to ensure the Department continues to make necessary progress;
- ◆ Requesting each Service and Defense Agency to provide me, within 90 days of the date of this memorandum, an implementation plan outlining its methodology to ensure we meet our commercial item acquisition goals; and
- ◆ Requesting that the IPT determine the feasibility of establishing a pilot program so that the Services and Agencies may collect market research and Commercial Item Determinations in a central database, or developing tools to assist in ensuring commercial item determinations are reasonably consistent. I request that the recommendation regarding this action be presented to DUSD (AR) within 90 days of the date of this memorandum.

The attachment provides some immediate clarification. In addition, DUSD (AR) and the components are developing a Commercial Item Handbook to provide further guidance on sound business strategies for acquiring commercial items. This guidebook is scheduled for release in February 2001.

To effectively provide our warfighters with the technological advantage to win future conflicts, we must uniformly look first to the commercial marketplace before developing new systems; upgrading legacy systems; or procuring spare parts and support services.

J. S. Gansler

Attachment:
As stated

CLARIFICATION OF FAR PART 12 FOR CONSISTENCY

In implementing the guidance of FAR Part 12, misinterpretations and/or inconsistent applications have occurred with regard to the following definitions and issues: commercial-off-the-shelf; modified commercial items; of a type; Government-off-the-shelf; market versus catalog price; requirements definition; conduct of market research; use of Commerce Business Daily (CBD) Note 26; and, sole-source situations. The following clarifications are offered to create consistency across the Department.

Commercial Off-the-Shelf (COTS): A product does not have to be commercial-off-the-shelf (COTS) to meet the "commercial item" definition. COTS items are a subset of commercial items. The commercial item definition is much broader than products that are presently available off- the-shelf. It includes items that have only been "offered" for sale, lease, or license to the general public, as well as those that have evolved from a commercial item and are offered for sale, even if not yet available in the commercial marketplace. However, evolved items must be available in the commercial marketplace in time to satisfy solicitation delivery requirements. In addition, all other elements of the commercial item definition at FAR 2.101 must also be met.

Modified Commercial Items: When items available in the commercial market cannot meet the Department's need, DoD must determine whether market items can be or have been modified so that FAR Part 12 can be used. Two types of modifications are available: (1) modifications of a type available in the commercial marketplace; and, (2) minor modifications of a type not customarily available in the commercial marketplace made to Federal Government requirements. For modifications of a type available in the commercial marketplace, the size or extent of modifications is unimportant. For minor modifications, the item must retain a predominance of nongovernmental functions or physical characteristics.

"Of a Type": The phrase "of a type" is not intended to allow the use of FAR Part 12 to acquire sole-source, military unique items that are not closely related to items already in the marketplace. Instead, "of a type" broadens the commercial item definition so that qualifying items do not have to be identical to those in the commercial marketplace. The best value offer in a competitive Part 12 solicitation can be an item that has previously satisfied the Government's need but has not been sold, leased, licensed, nor offered for sale, lease or license to the general public (a nondevelopmental item as defined in 10 USC 403 (13)). In this scenario, the phrase "of a type" allows the best value offer to qualify for a Part 12 contract as long as it is sufficiently like similar items that meet the government's requirement and are sold, leased, licensed, or offered for sale, lease or license to the general public. In such instances, "of a type" broadens the statutory commercial item definition to allow Part 12 acquisition of a government-unique item that can compete with commercial items that meet the government's requirement. This avoids the undesirable result of shutting out otherwise price-competitive preexisting suppliers of government-unique items from Part 12 solicitations.

Government Off-the-Shelf (GOTS): GOTS is a commonly used term for nondevelopmental items (NDI) (as defined in 10 USC 403 (13)) that are Government-unique items in use by a Federal Agency, a State or local government, or a foreign government with which the United States has a mutual defense cooperation agreement. The words "of a type" facilitate the acceptance of a best-value GOTS/NDI offer in response to a competitive FAR Part 12 solicitation when the offered GOTS/NDI items are sufficiently like similar items sold, leased, licensed, or offered for sale, lease or license to the general public.

Market Price versus Catalog Price for Services: The commercial item definition includes services of two general types: services in support of a commercial item; and, stand-alone services. In order to meet the commercial item definition, stand-alone services must be "based on established catalog or market prices." The price for the services must be based on either catalog prices or market prices.

> "Catalog Prices" mean a price included in a catalog, price list, schedule, or other form that is regularly maintained by the manufacturer or vendor, is either published or otherwise available for inspection by customers, and states prices at which sales are currently, or were last, made to a significant number of buyers constituting the general public.

> "Market Prices" mean current prices that are established in the course of ordinary trade between buyers and sellers free to bargain and that can be substantiated through competition or from sources independent of the offerors.

The established market price for stand-alone services does not have to be published or written. Market research enables the Government to collect data from independent sources in order to substantiate the market price.

Requirements Definition: It is imperative that all members of the acquisition team are cognizant of available or emerging technology and that requirement statements reflect any available commercial solutions. Requirements personnel and contracting officers should work together to ensure that commercial items can be -- and are -- used. Contracting officers need the input, guidance, and support of requirements personnel (e.g., adopting more open system architectures, identifying possible commercial components and technologies) to enable the use of commercial item acquisitions. The key to this process is robust market research.

Market Research: Market research -- and the teaming it relies upon -- must be an ongoing activity throughout an acquisition, in order to gather the robust data needed to make smart acquisition decisions. Market research is not limited to locating commercial items, although that is one purpose of its conduct. At a minimum, market research should be used to define requirements, locate commercial best practices, and assist in determining price reasonableness.

Full Use of CBD Note 26: If market research establishes that the Government's need cannot be met by a commercial item, FAR Part 12 shall not be used. For proposed contract actions that require publication in the Commerce Business Daily (CBD), the contracting officer must include a notice to prospective offerors that the Department does not intend to use FAR Part 12 for the acquisition. For the Defense Department, this notification is accomplished through use of CBD Numbered Note 26. The Department must make full use of CBD Numbered Note 26, which reads as follows:

> Based upon market research, the Government is not using the policies contained in Part 12, Acquisition of Commercial Items, in its solicitation for the described supplies or services. However, interested persons may identify to the contracting officer their interest and capability to satisfy the Government's requirement with a commercial item within 15 days of this notice.

Sole-Source Situations: Contracting officers and requirements personnel should work together to avoid sole-source situations. Competition is enabled when needs are broadly stated in terms of performance outcomes. However, a sole-source situation may be unavoidable, presenting pricing challenges. Tools and techniques are available for assisting in the price reasonableness determination for sole-source commercial item procurements. Sometimes, sole-source suppliers may attempt to exploit the lack of competitive markets and demand unreasonable prices. In such circumstances, the team should consider revising negotiation strategies to consider innovative solutions (e.g., strategic supplier alliances); buying the bare minimum quantities and working to restate the need to expand possible solutions and qualify alternate suppliers; and ultimately upgrading systems to current, commercial technology. In some cases, it may be necessary to escalate negotiations. The first escalation should be to the Procurement Executive, then, if necessary, to the Head of the Agency.

ESTABLISHMENT OF COMMERCIAL ITEM ACQUISITION GOALS

Commercial item acquisition using FAR Part 12 procedures is designed to provide greater access to commercial markets. Benefits include increased competition; use of market and catalog prices; and, access to leading edge technology and "non-traditional" business segments. The Road Ahead published on 2 June 2000 by USD (AT&L) established as a goal "an accelerated rate of increase in the dollar value of FAR Part 12 acquisitions with primes". The baseline is for this goal is $12.6 billion in FY 1999. Therefore, goals for Part 12 acquisitions are established for the components as follows:

1. Each Service and Defense Agency should double the dollar value of FAR Part 12 contract actions awarded in 1999 by the end of fiscal year (FY) 2005. This would bring the DoD total FAR Part 12 contract actions from $12.6 billion to $25.2 billion.*

2. Each Service and Defense Agency should strive to increase the number of FAR Part 12 contract actions awarded to 50 percent of all Government contract actions awarded by the end of FY 2005.*

(*For purposes of these goals, a contract action is defined as any new contract award and/or new delivery order placed against a contract awarded with a value greater than $25,000.)

While it is important to emphasize use of Part 12 acquisitions where appropriate, it is also important to balance these goals with the objectives to increase competition, achieve access to leading edge technologies and non-defense business segments. Therefore, in evaluating each of the goals established above, each Service and Defense Agency, together with DUSD (AR) should ensure that these objectives are not achieved at the expense of the use of product support requirements, use of strategic alliances, consolidated support service contracts or multiple award type contracts. These overlapping objectives may, unavoidably, create challenges for the components. These issues should be addressed in the implementation plans due to DUSD (AR) within 90 days. Specific activities, such as the Defense Logistics Agency, may also need to establish goals above these thresholds, depending on the nature of their business.

Appendix B
Definitions

COMMERCIAL ITEM (FEDERAL ACQUISITION REGULATION [FAR] 2.101)

(a) Any item, other than real property, that is of a type customarily used by the general public or by nongovernmental entities for purposes other than governmental purposes, and that—

    (1) Has been sold, leased, or licensed to the general public; or

    (2) Has been offered for sale, lease, or license to the general public;

(b) Any item that evolved from an item described in paragraph (a) of this definition through advances in technology or performance and that is not yet available in the commercial marketplace, but will be available in the commercial marketplace in time to satisfy the delivery requirements under a Government solicitation;

(c) Any item that would satisfy a criterion expressed in paragraphs (a) or (b) of this definition, but for—

    (1) Modifications of a type customarily available in the commercial marketplace; or

    (2) Minor modifications of a type not customarily available in the commercial marketplace made to meet Federal Government requirements. "Minor" modifications means modifications that do not significantly alter the nongovernmental function or essential physical characteristics of an item or component, or change the purpose of a process. Factors to be considered in determining whether a modification is minor include the value and size of the modification and the comparative value and size of the final product. Dollar values and percentages may be used as guideposts, but are not conclusive evidence that a modification is minor;

(d) Any combination of items meeting the requirements of paragraphs (a), (b), (c), or (e) of this definition that are of a type customarily combined and sold in combination to the general public;

(e) Installation services, maintenance services, repair services, training services, and other services if—

(1) Such services are procured for support of an item referred to in paragraph (a), (b), (c), or (d) of this definition, regardless of whether such services are provided by the same source or at the same time as the item; and

(2) The source of such services provides similar services contemporaneously to the general public under terms and conditions similar to those offered to the Federal Government;

(f) Services of a type offered and sold competitively in substantial quantities in the commercial marketplace based on established catalog or market prices for specific tasks performed under standard commercial terms and conditions. This does not include services that are sold based on hourly rates without an established catalog or market price for a specific service performed. For purposes of these services—

(1) "Catalog Price" means a price included in a catalog, price list, schedule, or other form that is regularly maintained by the manufacturer or vendor, is either published or otherwise available for inspection by customers, and states prices at which sales are currently, or were last, made to a significant number of buyers constituting the general public; and

(2) "Market Prices" mean current prices that are established in the course of ordinary trade between buyers and sellers free to bargain and that can be substantiated through competition or from sources independent of the offerors;(g) Any item, combination of items, or service referred to in paragraphs (a) through (f), notwithstanding the fact that the item, combination of items, or service is transferred between or among separate divisions, subsidiaries, or affiliates of a contractor; or

(h) A nondevelopmental item, if the procuring agency determines the item was developed exclusively at private expense and sold in substantial quantities, on a competitive basis, to multiple State and local governments.

COMMERCIALLY AVAILABLE OFF-THE-SHELF ITEM (FAR 2.101)

(a) Any item of supply—

(1) Other than real property, that is of a type customarily used by the general public or by nongovernmental entities for purposes other than governmental purposes, and that has been sold, leased, or licensed to the general public;

(2) That is sold, leased, or licensed in substantial quantities in the commercial marketplace; and(3) That is offered to the Government, without modification, in the same form in which it is sold, leased, or licensed in the commercial marketplace. Standard options are not modifications

(b) Does not include bulk cargo, as defined in 46 U.S.C. App. 1702, such as agricultural and petroleum products.

MARKET RESEARCH (FAR 2.101)

"Market research" is the process of collecting and analyzing information about capabilities within the market to satisfy agency needs.

NONDEVELOPMENTAL ITEM (FAR 2.101)

(a) Any previously developed item of supply used exclusively for governmental purposes by a Federal agency, a State or local government, or a foreign government with which the United States has a mutual defense cooperation agreement;

(b) Any item described in paragraph (a) of this definition that requires only minor modification or modifications of a type customarily available in the commercial marketplace in order to meet the requirements of the procuring department or agency; or

(c) Any item of supply being produced that does not meet the requirements of paragraph (a) or (b) solely because the item is not yet in use.

PRICE ANALYSIS (FAR 15.404-1(b))

Price analysis is the process of examining and evaluating a proposed price without evaluating its separate cost elements and proposed profit.

Appendix C
Commercial Item Definition Discussion

As a follow-up to the definition of "commercial item" set forth in Appendix B, the discussion below walks through this definition to discuss its subtleties.

Generally speaking, a commercial item is any item that is *of a type* that has been sold, leased, or licensed or even merely offered for sale, lease, or license to the general public. Several indicators of this are the existence of a commercial sales history, listings in catalogs or brochures, known established price, existence of multiple distributors, and availability or announcement to the general public.

The phrase "of a type" is not intended to allow the use of Federal Acquisition Regulation (FAR) Part 12 to acquire sole-source, military-unique items that are not closely related to items already in the marketplace. Rather, "of a type" broadens the commercial item definition so that qualifying items do not have to be identical to those in the commercial marketplace. The best-value offer in a competitive Part 12 solicitation can be for an item that has previously satisfied the Government's need but has not yet been sold, leased, licensed or offered for sale, lease, or license to the general public (e.g., a nondevelopmental item). In this scenario, the phrase "of a type" allows the best value offer to qualify for a Part 12 contract as long as the items offered are sufficiently like similar items that meet the Government's requirement and are sold, leased, licensed, or offered for sale, lease, or license to the general public. In such instances, "of a type" broadens the statutory commercial definition to allow Part 12 acquisition of a Government-unique item that can compete with commercial items that meet the Government's requirement. This avoids the undesirable result of preventing otherwise price-competitive preexisting suppliers of Government-unique items from responding to Part 12 solicitations.

Also included in the commercial item definition is any item that evolved from a commercial item as described above, through technical/performance advances—even if the item is not yet available in the commercial marketplace, as long as it will be available in time to satisfy the Government's requirements. Commercial items that evolve as a result of advances in technology or performance include product updates, model changes, and product improvements. For example, new versions of software fall into this category. Through this aspect of the "commercial item" definition, the Government can access new technology first.

A commercial item does not have to be "off-the-shelf" to be classified as commercial; items that require only modifications of a type customarily available in the commercial marketplace or minor Government-unique modifications still are considered commercial items. Thus, two types of modifications are available: (1) modifications of a type available in the commercial marketplace; and (2) minor modifications of a type not customarily available in the commercial marketplace, made to Federal Government requirements. For modifications of a type available in the commercial marketplace, the size or extent of the modifications is unimportant. For minor modifications, the item needs to retain a predominance of nongovernmental functions or essential physical characteristics. In either case, the source of funding for the modification does not impact its qualification as a commercial item.

In addition, the FAR definition of a "commercial item" also includes services. A service is considered a commercial item when it is provided in support of an item that meets the commercial item definition, or when the service itself is of a type offered and sold competitively in substantial quantities in the commercial market on the basis of established catalog or market prices for specific tasks performed under standard commercial terms and conditions. The latter, stand-alone definition does not preclude the inclusion of Government-unique requirements or terms and conditions, as long as there are sufficient "common characteristics" between the commercially available service and the service being acquired. Warehousing, garbage collection, and transportation of household goods are examples of services that are commercial. Other more sophisticated services (e.g., repair and overhaul work, research-related services, software design, testing, and engineering consultation) can also be commercial.

In order to meet the commercial item definition, the price for the stand-alone services must be "based on established catalog or market prices." The established market price for stand-alone services does not have to be published or written. Market research enables the Government to collect data from independent sources in order to substantiate the market price.

Although many Government systems are truly Government-unique items, this fact does not eliminate the need for acquisition professionals to promote the Government's preference for the procurement of commercial items. The commercial item definition is not limited to items acquired by the Government from prime contractors; it also includes commercial items acquired from subcontractors at all tiers, including items transferred from a contractor's divisions, affiliates, or subsidiaries.

Appendix D
Sample Commercial Item Checklist

Commercial Item Checklist
(Part 1: Items, Part 2: Services)

Item: _____

Part 1: Acquisition of Items

Can the Government's requirements (which should be performance based) be satisfied by—

1. An item that is *of a type* customarily used by the general public or by nongovernmental entities for purposes other than government purposes and that has been sold, leased, or licensed to the general public or that has been offered for sale, lease, or license to the general public?

A. If Yes, designate the item as commercial and annotate evidence of actual sale, lease, or license to the general public (or offer for the same), as appropriate:

_____

_____

B. If No, proceed.

2. An item that has evolved from an item described in 1 above through advances in technology or performance and that is not yet available in the commercial marketplace but will be available in time to satisfy the Government's delivery requirements?

A. If Yes, designate the item as commercial and annotate evidence that the item will be available in time to satisfy the Government's requirements.

_____

_____

B. If No, proceed.

3. An item that would meet 1 or 2 above but requires modifications of a type customarily available in the commercial marketplace or minor modifications of a type not customarily available in the commercial marketplace, made to meet Federal Government requirements?

A. If Yes, designate the item as commercial and annotate either evidence of the customary availability of modification in the commercial marketplace or the technical relationship between the modified item and the item that meets 1 or 2. (For the latter, attach drawings or comparison of the characteristics of the commercial item and the modified item, as appropriate).

_____

_____

B. If No, proceed.

4. Any combination of items meeting 1, 2, or 3 above that are of a type customarily combined and sold in combination to the general public?

    A. If Yes, designate the combination as commercial and annotate evidence of the customary combination being sold to the general public.

    _____

    _____

    B. If No, proceed.

5. Any item or combination of items that would meet 1, 2, 3, or 4 above but for being transferred between or among separate divisions, subsidiaries, or affiliates of a contractor?

    A. If Yes, designate the item as commercial and annotate how the item would meet 1, 2, 3, or 4.

    _____

    _____

    B. If No, proceed.

6. A nondevelopmental item that the procuring agency determines was developed exclusively at private expense and sold in substantial quantities, on a competitive basis, to multiple state and local governments?

A. If Yes, designate the nondevelopmental item as commercial and annotate evidence that it was 1) developed exclusively at private expense, and 2) sold competitively in substantial quantities to multiple state and local governments.

_____

_____

B. If No, recommend that the agency's requirements be revised to permit commercial solutions. If they cannot, recommend that noncommercial acquisition be considered (include Numbered Note 26 in the synopsis).

Part 2: Acquisition of Services

Can the Government's requirements be satisfied by—

1. Installation services, maintenance services, repair services, training services, and other services?

   A. If Yes, proceed to 2 below.

   B. If No, proceed to 4 below.

2. Services in 1 above in support of an item that has been, or could be, designated a commercial item in Part 1 above, regardless of whether such services are provided by the same source or at the same time as the item?

   A. If Yes, proceed to 3 below.

   B. If No, proceed to 4 below.

3. Services in 2 above from a source that provides similar services to the general public and the Government at the same time and under similar terms and conditions?

   A. If Yes, designate the services as commercial and annotate information concerning their source, as appropriate.

   _____

   _____

   B. If No, proceed to 4 below.

4. Services of a type offered and sold competitively in substantial quantities in the commercial marketplace

   A. If Yes, proceed to 5 below.

   B. If No, proceed to 7 below.

5. Services in 4 above for which the price is based on established catalog or market prices for specific tasks performed?

   A. If Yes, proceed to 6 below.

   B. If No, proceed to 7 below.

6. Services in 5 above that are offered under standard commercial terms and conditions?

   A. If Yes, designate the services as commercial and annotate pricing information, as appropriate.

D-3

_____
_____

    B. If No, proceed to 7 below.

7. Any combination of services that would meet 3 or 6 above but for being transferred between or among separate divisions, subsidiaries, or affiliates of a contractor?

    A. If Yes, designate the combination as commercial and annotate how the services would meet 3 or 6 above.

_____
_____

    B. If No, recommend that the agency's requirements be revised to permit commercial solutions. If they cannot, recommend that noncommercial acquisition be considered (include Numbered Note 26 in the synopsis).

Appendix E
Performance-Based Requirements Descriptions Resources

The following sources are available to provide information on performance-based statements of work:

- ◆ The Office of the Director, Defense Acquisition Initiatives offers the following information on its site at http://www.acq.osd.mil/ar/initiati.htm:

  - ➤ Performance Based Service Contracting (Training) Focus Group, Final Report, 22-23 April 1997

  - ➤ Executive Group II Workshop, 5 May 1997

  - ➤ Performance Based Service Contracting (Depot & Installation) Focus Group, Version One Report, 13 May 1997

  - ➤ Performance Based Service Contracting (Multiple Focus Groups), Final, 14-15 May 1997

  - ➤ Guidebook for Performance-Based Services Acquisition (PBSA) in the Department of Defense

- ◆ The Air Force Civil Engineer Support Agency offers a Library of Performance Work and Statements of Work in support of competitive sourcing at http://www.afcesa.af.mil/Directorate/CEO/Contracts/Outsourcing/.

- ◆ The Office of the Director, Defense Acquisition Initiatives offers a data warehouse of all of the Section 912(c) Reports, including *A Plan to Accelerate the Transition to Performance-Based: Report of the 912(c) Study Group for Review of the Acquisition Training, Processes, and Tools for Services Contracts* (June 1999). The report, which contains resources in its appendixes, is located at http://www.acq.osd.mil/ar/doc/servrpt.pdf.

- ◆ The National Association of Purchasing Managers and the National Contract Management Association teamed to offer online courses. Their *Performance-Based Service Acquisition* course (#3901) can be found at http://www.napm.org/Seminars/onlinecourses.cfm.

Appendix F
The Market Research Team

Using a team-based approach is the best way to effect market research. A market research team might take the form of an integrated product/process team (IPT). The following is a discussion of some of the relevant disciplines and what they can contribute to the market research effort.

USERS

Users drive the requirements forecast and formulate the long-term sustainment and provisioning over the entire life cycle. The Government can use this forecast information to develop favorable pricing throughout the program's life span, plan for modernization through spares, and negotiate terms for optimal management of inventory and distribution. Market research can provide insight into the total life-cycle requirements for similar systems, products, and/or processes using similar (or the same) commercial items. The information gathered from this research will permit users to conduct a comparative and parametric analysis to more accurately forecast total commercial item requirements.

PROGRAM OR PROJECT MANAGERS

Program or project managers are responsible for creating the program management plan, the acquisition strategy plan (the overarching plan that covers every contract and procurement for the program or project), the source selection plan, and the market research plan. They work hand in hand with contracting officers and specialists in organizing and planning the market research, addressing decisions such as who should conduct the actual research and who should comprise the market research team. Program or project managers identify how commercial items will fit into Government systems or programs.

ENGINEERS

Engineers make the decisions that principally drive the total cost of ownership. They also select the commercial items that will become part of (or will be needed to support) a system, product, and/or process. The engineering team usually designs, selects, and/or approves the use of a commercial item. Before systems engineers make this decision, they should conduct extensive market research to identify the full array of commercial items that may meet the requirement and try to select an item that will be commercially available from a multitude of sources. In addition, the engineers should consider the short- and long-term requirements of this item (e.g., product or process improvement, projected life cycle of the commercial item, and the source's commitment to its support and inventory). Engineers also assess items to determine whether they are "of a type" and whether essential physical characteristics would be changed by a modification. Furthermore, they help extrapolate engineering differences to support price analysis. Engineers evaluate features, options, and tradeoffs. They also revise the Government requirement as necessary to allow commercial items to meet their needs.

CONTRACT SPECIALISTS

Contract specialists receive training in market research. They work hand in hand with program or project managers on the organization and planning of the market research. The contract specialist usually works closely with the rest of the market research team in an effort to determine whether the commercial marketplace offers products that satisfy the agency's essential requirements, or that could satisfy them with some trade-offs or modifications. The contract specialist is also the individual whose in-depth understanding of the commercial item and the market environment is essential for evaluating the price of the commercial item. This knowledge helps determine whether the price is fair and reasonable, which offer represents the best value, and what terms and conditions are most appropriate.

PROGRAM BUDGET AND COST ANALYSTS

Program budget and cost analysts assist in forecasting the total cost of ownership. The program budget and cost analysts contribute to the DoD market research effort to determine whether other Government agencies are already ordering or using a commercial item. If so, those agencies can provide input on the item's quality, the market environment, pricing strategies used, and any unique aspects of their particular acquisition. This is particularly significant for sole-source commercial items. These analysts conduct cost tradeoff analysis (comparing commercial items to Government-unique items) and cost/benefit analysis (commercial versus Government approaches).

LOGISTICS SPECIALISTS

The involvement of logistics specialists during the concept and design phase of a program assures that lengthy and costly support requirements—after the system, product, or process is deployed—are considered in every design and development decision. Their contribution to the marketing research effort normally focuses on how effectively the proposed commercial spare parts can meet the long-term logistics requirements. To address this question, they research the length of time the commercial spare part will be manufactured, how the source plans to support the item (e.g., in terms of replacement parts, service, upgrades, product improvement), warranties, inventory management, packaging and distribution, and any specialized disposal requirements. These specialists conduct reliability/price tradeoff analysis.

OTHERS

Defense Contract Audit Agency auditors, Defense Contract Management Agency personnel, the small business advocate, and others can also play an important role on the market research team.

Appendix G
Sample Market Research Report

Sample Market Research Report Format

1.   Purchase Request (PR) # _____

2.   Title:_____

3.   Product or Service Code_____

4.   Estimated Contract Value (including options): $_____

5.   In accordance with Federal Acquisition Regulation (FAR) Part 10, market research has been conducted for this acquisition. The following techniques were used (check all that apply):

_____Historical acquisition information (review of recent market research results for similar or identical supplies/services). (See Appendix H for more detail).

_____Personal knowledge in procuring supplies/services of this type.

_____Contact with the requester and/or other knowledgeable people in Government and industry regarding the commercial nature of this requirement and standard industry practices in this area of supply/service.

_____Publication of a formal request for information on the Internet .

_____Publication of a formal request for information through the Government-wide point of entry.

_____Publication in appropriate technical journals.

_____Review of Government and/or commercial databases for relevant information.

_____Review of Internet resources, such as the Commercial Advocates Forum Web site (see http://www.cadv.org for relevant information).

_____Use of source lists for identical or similar items obtained from Government, professional, and/or industry sources.

_____Review of catalogs and other generally available product literature (online and/or in hard copy).

_____Interchange meetings or presolicitation conferences with potential offerors.

_____Other:_____

6.   On the basis of the results of the above research (and on the information in Appendix D), it is determined that this requirement:

_____*Can* be met by commercial items, commercial items with customary or minor modifications, or nondevelopmental items.

OR

_____*Cannot* be met by commercial items, commercial items with modifications, or nondevelopmental items. Further, a reevaluation has been made in accordance with FAR 10.002(b), and the Government requirement cannot be modified in a way that will allow a commercial item to meet the need. *Note:* Any presolicitiaton synopsis of this requirement must include Numbered Note 26.

OR

_____Other:

_____
_____
_____

(Example: Market research may reveal that a combination of commercial/noncommercial items can meet the Government's needs.)

7.   Synopsize the reasons for the determination in 6:

_____
_____
_____
_____
_____
_____
_____
_____

Address numbers 8 through 11 below if the requirement can be met (either in whole or in part) by commercial items, commercial items with modifications, or nondevelopmental items.

Continue on additional sheets if necessary.

8. Pricing factors (e.g., pricing history, competitive conditions, overall level of demand, trends in supply and demand, pattern of demand, other impacting market forces, pricing strategies, sources of supplies): (See Appendix M for more information.)

    _____
    _____
    _____
    _____

9. Standard industry terms and conditions (e.g., warranty, maintenance, discounts, buyer financing, freight, delivery, acceptance/rejection) under which commercial sales of the required supplies/services are made:

    _____
    _____
    _____
    _____

10. Laws or regulations unique to the required supplies/services:

    _____
    _____
    _____
    _____

11. On the basis of the above information, the basic clauses and provisions prescribed in FAR Part 12:

    _____Are sufficient for use in this acquisition and do not require any substantial tailoring to be consistent with industry's commercial practices.

    OR

    _____Require tailoring to be consistent with industry's commercial practices. All such tailoring will be included in the solicitation issued for the required supplies/services.

Signed: _____ (Contracting Officer)

Date: _____

Signed: _____ (Program Manager or User)

Date: _____

Appendix H
Market Research Questions—Historical Acquisition Information

The table presented below sets forth research elements the Government should consider when market research is completed. Not all of the questions in this table will be valid for every acquisition. For some acquisitions, many specialized questions not covered in the table will need to be answered. However, the topics identified and the related questions provide a good framework for use when reviewing historical acquisition information.

Historical Acquisition Information	
Research Element	**Be Able to Answer Questions Such As...**
Trends in Supply and Demand	• When did past acquisitions take place? • Is there any indication of prevailing market conditions at that time?
Pattern of Demand	• What quantities were solicited for each acquisition? • What quantities were acquired?
Sources of Supplies or Services	• How many sources were solicited for the prior acquisition? • What specific sources were solicited? • How many sources made offers? • What specific sources made offers?
Product Characteristics	• Are there any significant differences between the Government requirements documents for the prior contract and the current requirements?
Delivery/ Performance Terms	• What was the delivery or performance period in days, weeks, months, or years? • In what month(s) were the supplies to be delivered or the services to be performed? • Did the contractor meet the delivery targets? • What was the free on board (f.o.b.) point? • Was premium transportation required for timely delivery?
Ownership Costs	• What costs of ownership were associated with the acquisition?
Acquisition Method	• What acquisition method was employed for past acquisitions?
Contract Terms and Conditions	• What were the general terms of past contracts? • Are there any significant differences between the terms of the last contract (e.g., packing requirements, type of contract, and the like) and those recommended for this acquisition?
Problems	• What problems (if any) were encountered during contract performance?

Appendix I
Market Research Resources

The following sources are available to assist with market research efforts. Many other sources of market information pertaining to particular industries and products are available.

TUTORIALS AND GUIDES

- The Defense Logistics Agency offers a *Market Research* handbook (SD-5) through http://www.dsp.dla.mil/documents/sd-5.html.

- The Federal Acquisition Institute offers an online *Acquisition Planning* course; Lesson 2 is dedicated to market research. The online course is located at http://www.faionline.com/fai/register_new/fai_main.asp.

- The Federal Acquisition Institute offers an online *Market Research* course. The course is available at http://www.faionline.com/fai/register/main_frm.htm.

- The Navy's Acquisition Reform Office offers a *Market Research* tutorial at http://www.acq-ref.navy.mil/tools/marketresearch/index.html.

- The National Aeronautics and Space Administration, Office of Procurement, offers a *Market Research Guide* at http://www.hq.nasa.gov/office/procurement/market.html.

- The U.S. Department of Commerce, Bureau of Export Administration, offers *Defense Market Reports* at http://www.doc-bxa.bmpcoe.org/dmrr.html.

- The National Association of Purchasing Management offers several products and seminars at http://www.napm.org.

- The National Contract Management Association offers several publications and seminars at http://www.ncmahq.org.

PRODUCT AND INDUSTRY DATA SOURCES

- Commercial procurement information services. Several subscription services provide procurement and logistics information via the Internet. The type of information offered includes specifications and standards, technical descriptions, and procurement history (e.g., contract numbers, date procured, unit prices). Since these services contain procurement information from the Army, Navy, Air Force, and other procurement organizations, subscribers can obtain a wider range of information than would normally be available from in-house databases. In addition to providing a single point of entry for querying various Government databases, these services also include nongovernmental information (e.g., supplier catalogs).

◆ Thomas Register. Thomas Register (which is published both in print and on the Internet at http://www.thomasregister.com) consists of an alphabetical listing of American and Canadian companies, addresses, and phone numbers, as well as a product listing, product description, and product manufacturers. The Thomas Register can be searched by company name, product or service, or brand name, and the search can be modified to limit it to a specific geographical area. For example, searching under the product "nails" will yield a list of "Product Headings" to help narrow down the type of nails, such as "nails: collated," "nails: galvanized," or "nails: drywall." Searches can also be performed by the name of a company that distributes nails, such as Hahn Systems, Inc. Alternatively, a search for nails can be done by citing a particular manufacturer (i.e., brand name), such as Powers Rawl.

◆ Thomas Register's TREND® Online. This site (http://www.trendonline.com) provides buyers and specifiers with over 400,000 industrial and commercial suppliers, organized under more than 4,500 product and service categories.

◆ Consumer Price Index. The Consumer Price Index (CPI) is published monthly by the U.S. Department of Labor's Bureau of Labor Statistics, with Internet-based information found at http://www.bls.gov/cpi/. The CPI represents changes in prices of all goods and services purchased for consumption by urban households. It measures price change from the perspective of the buyer, in contrast to the Producer Price Index (PPI), which measures price change from the seller's perspective. A primary use of the CPI is to adjust income and expenditure streams for changes in the cost of living. The CPI is used as a price adjustment factor in some areas of procurement (leasing, in particular) and as a general gauge for inflation. However, the PPI is usually a better source of data on price trends for the Government, since the Government is usually a "wholesale" buyer.

◆ Producer Price Index. The PPI is a family of indexes published by the U.S. Department of Labor's Bureau of Labor Statistics, with Internet-based information found at http://www.bls.gov/ppi/. It tracks changes in prices that producers receive from the initial commercial purchasers of their products. The Index reflects selling prices of selected manufacturers or the prices quoted on organized exchanges such as the Chicago Board of Trade. Prices are generally free on board (f.o.b.) origin for immediate delivery. A primary use of the PPI is to deflate revenue streams in order to measure real growth in output. The PPI measures price change from the perspective of the seller, in contrast to other measures (such as the CPI), that measure price change from the purchaser's perspective. Sellers' and purchasers' prices may differ as a result of Government subsidies, sales and excise taxes, and distribution costs. The individual indexes of the PPI, which are helpful for conducting price analysis, are used in the following ways, among others:

➤ As an economic indicator.

- ➤ As a deflator of other economic series.

- ➤ As the basis for contract escalation.

- ◆ Acquisition Reform Net, http://www.arnet.gov.

- ◆ BizWeb, http://www.bizweb.com.

- ◆ Commercial Advocates Forum, http://www.cadv.org.

- ◆ Department of Commerce, http://www.stat-usa.gov/.

- ◆ Department of Defense EMALL, http://www.emall.dla.mil/.

- ◆ Dow Jones Business Information Services, http://www.dowjones.com

- ◆ Federal Supply Schedule, http://www.fss.gsa.gov.

- ◆ General Services Administration (GSA) *Advantage!,* http://www.gsaadvantage.gov/.

- ◆ ITEC Direct offers U. S. Navy standard compliant Information Technology (IT) products and services from several GSA Federal Supply Schedule contractors, http://www.itec-direct.navy.mil/index.shtml.

- ◆ Javits-Wagner-O'Day, http://www.jwod.com.

- ◆ Manufacturer's Information Network, http://mfginfo.com/home.htm.

- ◆ National Association of Purchasing Management, http://www.napm.org.

- ◆ National Contract Management Association, http://www.ncmahq.org.

- ◆ Product: Aircraft

  - ➤ Internet Parts Locator System, http://www.ipls.com.

  - ➤ Spec2000, http://www.spec2000.com.

- ◆ Product: Apparel, Fiber, Textiles

  - ➤ Garment Industry Development Corporation, http://www.gidc.org/.

- ◆ Product: Computers and Electronics

  - ➤ Electronic Industries Association, http://www.eia.org.

  - ➤ Price Watch, http://www.pricewatch.com.

  - ➤ TechnoGate, http://www.technogate.com.

- Small Business Administration, http://www.sba.gov.

- Standard and Poor's Research Reports, http://www.researchmag.com.

- Tech Savvy, http://www.techsavvy.com.

- Yellow Pages, http://www.bigyellow.com and http://www.switchboard.com.

Appendix J
Categories Related to Commercial Items

The following categories are related to commercial items, but they are not synonymous. The fact that an item/service to be procured does not easily fit into the nondevelopmental item (NDI) or Government off-the-shelf (GOTS) categories does not in itself mean that it is not a commercial item:

◆ Commercial off-the-shelf (COTS) items,

◆ NDIs, and

◆ GOTS items.

COMMERCIAL OFF-THE-SHELF ITEMS

COTS items are commercial items that have been sold, leased, or licensed in substantial quantities in the commercial marketplace and that are offered to the Government without modification. The COTS definition does not include services or bulk cargo, such as agricultural and petroleum products. A product does not have to be COTS to meet the "commercial item" definition. COTS items are a subset of commercial items. The commercial item definition is much broader and embraces products other than those that are presently available off the shelf. It includes items that have only been "offered" for sale, lease, or license to the general public—the items do not need to have been actually sold, leased, or licensed yet. It also includes items that have evolved from a commercial item and are offered for sale, even if they are not yet available in the commercial marketplace. However, only evolved items that will be available in the commercial marketplace in time to satisfy the delivery requirements stated in the solicitation meet the "commercial item" definition. In addition, all other elements of the commercial item definition at FAR 2.101 must also be met.

NONDEVELOPMENTAL ITEMS

Nondevelopmental items (NDIs) are considered commercial items if the procuring agency determines that they were developed exclusively at private expense and sold in substantial quantities on a competitive basis to multiple state and local governments.

GOVERNMENT OFF-THE-SHELF ITEMS

"GOTS" is a commonly used term for NDIs that are Government-unique items in use by a Federal agency, a state or local government, or a foreign government with which the United States has a mutual defense cooperation agreement. The words "of a type" facilitate the acceptance of a best-value GOTS/NDI offer in response to a competitive FAR Part 12 solicitation when the offered GOTS/NDI items are sufficiently like similar items sold, leased, or licensed, or offered for sale, lease, or license, to the general public.

Appendix K
Alternative Approaches to Commercial Item Determinations

Title VIII of the Federal Acquisition Streamlining Act sets forth the statutory requirements for acquiring commercial items. Section 2377 of the Act specifies a preference for commercial item acquisitions. Section 8105 specifies that certain provisions of law do not apply to acquisitions of items that meet the definition of a commercial item. Further, Section 8002 limits the types of clauses that may be included in a contract for an item meeting the statutory commercial item definition. Federal Acquisition Regulation (FAR) implementation of the Act provided acquisition officials with wide latitude to use judgment in deciding whether a Government need can be met by an item that meets the commercial item definition. However, neither the Act itself nor the FAR implementation specifies how this decision is to be made or at what level of an organization it is to be made. To implement the Act's requirements consistently, alternative approaches to commercial item determinations should be considered. Consistency should exist across the Department in the approach to acquiring supplies and services that are obviously commercial.

PRIOR AGENCY OR DEPARTMENT DETERMINATIONS

When Government acquisition personnel have previously determined that an item meets the commercial item definition and have used commercial item policies and procedures to acquire the item, it is usually not necessary to repeat a full-scale commerciality determination in subsequent acquisitions of the same item in similar circumstances. However, it is important that contracting officers examine a previous determination if there is reason to believe that market conditions have changed significantly. Any decision to overturn a previous commercial/noncommercial determination by any Government agency must be documented as such.

IDENTIFYING GROUPS OF ITEMS AS COMMERCIAL

Whenever possible, logical groupings of items should be identified as "commercial" without conducting an individual technical review of every item. This strategy is critical for significantly accelerating the pace at which items can be identified as commercial, because the resources needed to conduct individual item reviews are being steadily reduced. The contracting officer retains authority to make a final determination on each item but would not be required to examine the recommendation unless there was reason to question it. Some examples of items that could logically be presumed to be commercial are as follows

- ◆ Items for which industry standards (ASTM, SAE, etc.) are used as the sole procurement document.

- Items described by commercial item descriptions (CIDs).

- Items with Acquisition Method Suffix Code (AMSC) "Z" (see DoD FAR Supplement [DFARS] Appendix E, Part 2, Breakout Coding), *if* the contracting activity buys virtually all nondevelopmental items. (AMSC Z includes commercial, nondevelopmental, and off-the-shelf items.).

- Federal Stock Classes (FSCs) that can reasonably be presumed to be commercial, such as lumber, specified metals, subsistence, medical, and fuel.

Congressional Mandates

Congress can declare that procurements of certain classes of items should be treated as procurements of commercial items. For example, the National Defense Authorization Act for Fiscal Year 2000 included provisions authorizing DoD to conduct a five-year pilot program treating the procurement of certain commercial services (utilities and housekeeping, education and training, and medical services) as procurements of commercial items. During the pilot program, these classes of services are automatically subject to the streamlined guidance of FAR Part 12. The pilot program is designed to test the concept of treating certain classes of services as commercial items (in contrast to the current individual contract determinations, which will continue to occur for all other classes of services). Congress will use the data gathered from this pilot program for any future decisions on using class determinations for commercial items.

In addition, the Floyd D. Spence National Defense Authorization Act for Fiscal Year 2001 included a provision that allows DoD to treat performance-based service contracts/task orders valued at $5 million or less as commercial items if certain conditions are met.

Contractor Determinations

Prime contractors and subcontractors at all tiers are required to incorporate, to the maximum extent practicable, commercial items or nondevelopmental items as components of items supplied to agencies. Contractors make commercial item determinations in much the same way Government acquisition personnel do. Interchange between Government and industry on this topic is encouraged because it is mutually beneficial.

Contractor determinations are another source of information that acquisition personnel should consider when making their own commercial item determinations. If a contractor procured an item commercially, and the Government subsequently acquires the same item, acquisition personnel should consider the contractor's determination as part of their own market research efforts. Likewise, if the Government determines that an item is commercial, the prime contractor should consider the Government's determination as part of its own market research efforts.

Agency Class Determinations

An effort is under way within the Department to encourage each military service/agency to designate specific categories or classes of items/services as commercial. Doing so would avoid the need to make these decisions repetitively—and perhaps inconsistently—within an agency.

An example of a possible class commerciality determination is the designation of a particular Federal Supply Code (FSC), by a service or agency head, as commercial. Current authority allows activity heads and department/division/branch heads to make class determinations for FSCs. Any such determination should be appropriately documented in accordance with activity procedures.

Corporate Council Agreements

Several companies have formed corporate councils[1] to provide an interface between company representatives and senior DoD leadership. These councils are designed to provide leadership for corporate-wide initiatives, strengthen the relationship with DoD, and elevate Single Process Initiatives (SPI) proposals for corporate-wide endorsement and implementation. Corporate councils can also facilitate the resolution of disagreements, encourage consensus, and identify and resolve issues. The councils offer DoD an opportunity to communicate with key suppliers on global acquisition reform initiatives. A corporate council, in conjunction with DoD, could make a determination, based on research available at the time of the determination, that certain items acquired by DoD meet the definition of commercial items. These determinations may appear in the DFARS.

Commercial Facilities

Evidence that an item is produced in a facility predominately engaged in producing similar items for the commercial market, or on a production line that produces similar items for the commercial market, is one indication that the item being acquired may be a commercial item. Such evidence could be provided by a potential supplier and corroborated through market research.

When such facilities are identified, products procured from them are candidates for agency class determinations, as discussed above, or facility-wide determinations.

---

[1] For more information on corporate councils, see the 14 September 1999 memorandum of Dr. Jacques S. Gansler, Under Secretary of Defense (Acquisition, Technology and Logistics), available at http://www.acq.osd.mil/ar/docs/councils.pdf.

Appendix L
Market Research—Pricing Information Sources

Market research can be used to locate many sources for pricing information. They include the following:

◆ Supplier catalogs.

◆ Electronic Internet search engines such as Yahoo, Excite, Google, All the Web, Lycos, and Infoseek.

◆ Government "electronic malls."

◆ Data readily available from market research (comparative information regarding competitors and the competitive environment).

◆ Data available from Government purchasing/engineering activities (purchase history, engineering estimates, etc.).

◆ Analogies—comparative pricing information for similar items.

◆ Parametric analyses (rough yardstick correlation based on thrust, range, processing speed, weight, or other technical factors or item characteristics).

◆ Advice from Government pricing and audit personnel.

◆ Company historical records.

◆ Industry association databases.

Each Government market research effort will be different because of requirements specific to the procurement, varying market conditions, and other factors. For example, in buying a new office computer system, the Government would certainly want to know comparative prices across the marketplace for computers with the state of technology and equipment the Government anticipates buying. Further, the Government would want to know the various suppliers' warranty provisions. The Government would also need to know what the life-cycle costs would be for any given system. In other words, software costs, costs for disposal of old equipment, training costs, and the costs for site preparation, for example, should be calculated.

If the Government were buying batteries, such as 1.5 volt alkaline batteries, then the pricing factors considered in market research might differ. For example, here the Government would want to consult catalogs readily available in the marketplace to determine various manufacturers' prices. What are their practices for offering quantity discounts? What about the quality of the batteries? Answers to these questions would determine the market niche for price comparisons and other factors. The Government also would want to consider supplier delivery terms and conditions. Finally, the Government would consider environmental factors—are the batteries environmentally safe, and do they cause increased costs due to unique disposal requirements?

The Government's considerations in buying a major aircraft, like a Boeing 757, which could be modified for military purposes, would differ from the examples presented above. In this instance, the Government would want to develop a pricing algorithm for the basic aircraft plus the modifications the Government requires, which would consider the plane's weight, lift, fuel consumption, range, noise, and cube (space). These are the kinds of things the Government would have to consider during the estimation process and proposal evaluation. Another very important issue for the Government to consider is the state of technology. This will give the Government the knowledge of the comparative "value" of the plane in the marketplace. Is the technology sunrise or sunset? Additionally, information about maintenance costs is needed for evaluating the life-cycle costs and savings. Warranty on the aircraft, and the speed with which the Government can expect aircraft deliveries, are also important considerations.

Appendix M
Market Research Questions—Price-Related Information

The table below identifies the type of price-related questions that the Government should be able to answer when market research is completed. Not all of the questions in this table will be valid for every acquisition. For some acquisitions, many specialized questions not covered in the table will need to be answered. However, the topics identified and the related questions provide a good framework for market research. Market research should continue throughout the entire acquisition process, up to and including the conclusion of negotiations.

Pricing Factors to Consider in Market Research	
Research Factor	**Be Able to Answer Questions Such As...**
Pricing History	• What information is available concerning past prices paid for the service or item of supply and about changes in the supply item or service or market since then? • Have there been historic differences between prices paid by the Government vis-à-vis other buyers? Why?
Competitive Conditions	• How many sellers are in the market? • How many buyers? • Are other companies expected to enter the market?
Overall Level of Demand	• What is the relationship of the quantity the Government intends to buy vis-à-vis the quantities that others buy? • Will the planned volume justify a lower-than-market price as a result of the seller's increased economies of scale? • Will the planned volume be so large as to drive the sellers to or beyond full capacity, resulting in unanticipated inflation? • Is the procurement for items at the leading edge of market demand (i.e., market demand is increasing), or at the back end (i.e., demand for the item is dropping)?
Trends in Supply and Demand	• Will demand be higher or lower at the time of award than now? • Will supply capacity keep pace with demand?
Pattern of Demand	• Is there a cyclical pattern to supply and demand? • Would awarding six months from now result in lower prices than an immediate award? Or would it be better to stock up now at today's prices?
Other Market Forces Expected to Affect Contract Price	• What forces might drive up prices in the near future? Strikes? Labor shortages? Subcontractor bottlenecks? Energy shortages? Other raw material shortages? • What forces might lead the Government to expect lower prices in the future?
Pricing Strategies	• What are the pricing strategies of firms in the market?

	• What are the implications for expected prices? • Are discounts available for quantity buys?
Sources of Supplies or Services	• Which firms in the market are the most likely to submit offers to a Government solicitation? • Which are the least likely, and why?
Supply or Service Characteristics	• What features distinguish one service or item of supply from another? • Which commercial supplies or services match most closely the Government requirements document (as it currently reads in the purchase request)? • What is the apparent trade-off between features and price?
Delivery/ Performance Terms	• What are the current distribution channels? • What are current transportation costs (if available and applicable)? • What are the commercial lead-times?
Ownership Costs	• What are the commercial warranty terms and conditions (if any)? • What are the historical repair costs for each item? • What are the historical maintenance costs for each item?
Contract Terms and Conditions	• What terms and conditions are used in commercial transactions for the supply item or service? • What terms and conditions have been used in other Government acquisitions of the supply item or service? • What type of contract is generally used in commercial transactions for the supply item or service? Government acquisitions?
Problems	• What has been the historical default rate by firms performing similar contracts? • What performance problems have typically been encountered? • Have similar acquisitions been characterized by claims or cost overruns?
Overall Value	• What is the relationship between price and the overall value to the Government?

Appendix N
Price Analysis Techniques

Price analysis techniques include the following:

◆ Comparison of proposed prices received in response to the solicitation. Normally, adequate price competition may be used as the basis for a price reasonableness determination. However, it is important that the file document that the competition was "adequate" to ensure that the award price is fair and reasonable.

◆ Comparison of previously proposed prices and previous Government and commercial contract prices with current proposed prices for the same or similar items, if both the validity of the comparison and the reasonableness of the previous price(s) can be established. For example, circumstances may have compelled the Government to pay a price that could not be determined fair and reasonable; such prices should not be used for future price comparisons unless additional information subsequently becomes available to establish that the price paid was indeed fair and reasonable. The agency may have past experience acquiring the same or similar items. Using past prices as a baseline, a buyer can evaluate the current price, looking for a rational explanation for any unusual price movements. All relevant previous price history should be used, not just the most recent price.

◆ Use of parametric estimating methods/application of rough yardsticks (such as dollars per pound or per horsepower, or other units) to highlight significant inconsistencies that warrant additional pricing inquiry. Parametric estimating methods are useful in establishing price reasonableness for sole-source items. Cost-estimating relationships (CERs) are used to develop parametric estimates. A CER is a formula for estimating prices on the basis of the relationship of past prices with one or more product physical or performance characteristics. Whenever item price can be related to the value of one or more physical or performance characteristics, that relationship can be used to estimate the price of a similar product. For example, builders commonly estimate the price of a planned building by multiplying the number of square feet in the building by an estimated cost per square foot.

◆ Comparison with competitive published price lists, published market prices of commodities, similar indexes, and discount or rebate arrangements. One published price list is a supplier's catalog. (When using a catalog price, Government buyers should consider whether the large size of a Government buy could enable substantial volume discounts.) The fact that a price is included in a catalog does not, in and of itself, make it fair and reasonable. The Government should obtain information concerning standard discounts and discounts for larger quantities or improved or reduced levels of services and negotiate a reasonable price accordingly.

◆ Comparison of proposed prices with independent Government estimates. (For detailed information on independent Government estimates, see the Contract Pricing Reference Guide at http://hydra.gsa.gov/staff/v/guides/ VOL2-97.pdf.) Every independent Government estimate should address the following:

> ➤ How the estimate was made.

> ➤ What assumptions were made.

> ➤ What information and tools were used.

> ➤ The source of the information used.

> ➤ How previous estimates compared with prices paid.

◆ Comparison of proposed prices with prices obtained through market research for the same or similar items.

◆ Analysis of pricing information provided by the offeror.

If information is necessary to support further analysis, the following order of preference should generally be used:

◆ Price information obtained from within the Government.

◆ Price information obtained from sources other than the offeror (e.g., sources of market information discussed in this Handbook).

◆ Price information obtained from the offeror.

◆ Cost information (i.e., information that does not meet the definition of cost or pricing data) obtained from the offeror.

In any event, a request for information from an offeror should be limited to information in the form regularly maintained by the offeror as part of its commercial operations.

Appendix O
Achieving Fair and Reasonable Prices for Sole-Source Items

A variety of techniques may be useful in achieving fair and reasonable prices when the Government has only a minimum of market leverage. The absence of market leverage can make the task more difficult regardless of whether an item is commercial. By following the guidance in this Handbook, the Government acquisition team will place itself in the best possible position to achieve outcomes that are in the Government's best interest.

PRICE REASONABLENESS DIFFICULTIES

When having difficulty achieving price reasonableness in a sole-source situation, consider using the following techniques:

- ◆ Revise the negotiation to consider innovative solutions.

- ◆ Escalate the negotiation (the first escalation should be to the procurement executive, then, if necessary, to the head of the agency).

- ◆ Buy minimum quantities and qualify alternative solutions or suppliers.

- ◆ Work with requirements personnel to restate the need in order to expand available solutions.

- ◆ Upgrade systems to current, commercial technology.

Requiring activities should adapt to and leverage the commercial marketplace, rather than expecting the commercial marketplace to adapt to the DoD environment. Suppliers striving to preserve their commercial practices should not be considered unreasonable solely on that basis.

EXAMPLE: CONTRACTOR X

In 1997, the DoD Inspector General (IG) criticized the Defense Logistics Agency (DLA) for paying excessive prices for sole-source commercial items from contractor X. The actions identified were individual purchase orders, contracts, and delivery orders against basic ordering agreements awarded from 1994 through 1996 for various aircraft spare parts. Even though the prices paid were 20 percent lower than the catalog prices that commercial customers paid, they were an average of 280 percent higher (adjusted for inflation) than prices previously paid by the Government (prior to 1994, when most of the items did not meet the commercial item definition). In other words, absent any additional value being offered by the contractor (there was none) to offset the higher prices, the fact that DLA was paying less than every commercial customer and 20 percent less than catalog price was not adequate to determine the prices to be fair and reasonable.

Even after the IG identified its concerns, the contractor was not willing to negotiate lower prices for these items when purchased individually. This remained true even when the procurements were elevated to the command level at the buying activity. However, the contractor did agree to negotiate a "corporate contract" for all items in its commercial catalog. In other words, the grouping of many smaller requirements into a larger, long-term contract made DLA a more attractive business partner to X, and X was willing to negotiate a better deal because there was something beneficial in it for the contractor.

DLA conducted extensive market research on the items involved and used a variety of price analyses to discretely price as many of the individual items as possible. Market research led to alternative sources for a few of the items. DLA awarded a contract for 216 items in X's commercial catalog at prices averaging about 71 percent lower than catalog prices. Again, a percentage off a catalog price does not necessarily mean anything in terms of price reasonableness. Using the IG's methodology of comparison to previous prices showed that the new prices were still 40 percent higher than the pre-1994 prices. However, DLA achieved significant administrative and inventory cost savings that can be attributed to administrative lead-time savings (over 100 days per order saved) and those gained by awarding delivery orders against the corporate contract instead of making individual awards. In other words, while the unit prices were higher than those the Government had paid in the past, savings in other costs to the Government offset the increased unit prices.

This example illustrates how the Government can secure value through corporate contracting in ways that cannot be accomplished just by focusing on a particular item. When corporate contracting is used to secure value, it is important that file documentation clearly communicate to future buyers what the price represents (e.g., the business considerations that affected the instant price) so that they will understand the specifics before they attempt to use the information in future awards.

Appendix P
Configuration Control and Logistics Support

The Government is giving contractors configuration control at higher and higher levels of the "system" in order to insert advanced technologies faster and at lower cost.

The degrees of contractor configuration control and logistics support should relate to total cost, performance, and risk. For example, in the past, the Government maintained a large infrastructure to support organic supply and maintenance. Now contractors often support equipment. This arrangement not only shifts these activities to the competitive private sector, it also enables technology insertion that enhances capability. Over a typical weapon system life cycle, maintaining and supporting original technology can cost much more than inserting new technology in an evolutionary manner. It is important that the cost savings comprise all costs, including Government overhead costs as well as direct program costs.

In general, the Government should *not* stock spares in excess of those adequate for reasonable response times, but rather embrace new concepts of supply chain management, including just-in-time inventories, direct supplier delivery, and contractor-held inventories. Instead of managing supplies, Government managers should be managing suppliers and their performance.

The best way to protect source availability and avoid diminishing sources is to have a program of continuous technology upgrades. This can be accomplished by sustaining commercial engineering, value engineering incentive programs, and well-defined interfaces.

Program managers should act early in the product life cycle to mitigate source-of-supply risks. These risks include business dissolution, product line elimination, and quality degradation. Actions that can reduce these risks include placing design drawings in escrow with a third party in case a supplier discontinues production, negotiating contract terms that require the provision of design drawings to the Government if the business dissolves, and negotiating contract terms that require prior notice and provide options for product life buyout if production of an item ends. Since lifetime buys are very expensive, they should not necessarily be made for the program's duration, but rather should be employed as an interim measure until a technology insertion strategy unfolds.

If all of these approaches are inadequate and sources of supply are threatened, DoD has programs for managing diminishing manufacturing sources of supply. These programs exchange information and identify alternatives for those faced with supply-base problems. One such effort is the Virtual Parts Supply Base project (http://www.vpsb.com). Another is the Air Force's Diminishing Manufacturing Sources and Material Shortages (DMSMS) Program (http://www.ml.afrl.af.mil/ib/dpdsp/dmsms.htm). Also, the Government–Industry Data Exchange Program (GIDEP) (http://www.gidep.corona.navy.mil/mgmt/pm.htm) supports this communication process.

Appendix Q
Pricing-Support Resources

The following sources are available to provide pricing support:

- The Army's report entitled *Constructing Successful Business Relationships: Innovation in Contractual Incentives* is available at http://acqnet.saalt.army.mil/library/default.htm.

- The Air Force's guide entitled *Award Fee and Award Term Guide* is available at http://www.afmc.wpafb.af.mil/HQ-AFMC/PK/pkp/pkpc/awardfee.htm.

- The Federal Acquisition Institute and the Air Force Institute of Technology offer *The Contract Pricing Reference Guides* at http://www.gsa.gov/fai.

- The Defense Contract Management Agency's One Book offers guidance at http://www.dcma.mil/.

- The U.S. Navy PRICE FIGHTERS is a specialized organization that exists to provide negotiation support. It can be reached via e-mail at price_fighters@fossac.navy.mil.

- The Federal Acquisition Institute offers an online *Market Research* course. The course has a section on developing price estimates that strongly emphasizes awareness of (1) changes in quantity discounts that can affect prices; (2) current market conditions, such as the extent to which increased competition can lower prices; and (3) effects resulting from changes from detailed design specifications to performance requirements enabling consideration of new sources that may lead to lower prices. The course is available at http://www.faionline.com/fai/register/main_frm.htm.

- The Office of the Deputy Under Secretary of Defense (Acquisition Reform) sponsored two satellite broadcasts in an educational program on commercial pricing and contracting in a sole-source environment:

  - *Contract Pricing One* was held on February 25, 1998. This program addressed tools and techniques for determining fair market value and prices for commercial items.

  - *Contract Pricing Two* was held on June 25, 1998. This program addressed tools and commercial practices for obtaining fair and reasonable prices in both competitive and sole-source environments.

Information about satellite broadcasts can be found at http://www.dau.mil/. The broadcasts were offered through the Acquisition Reform Communications Center (ARCC) (a directorate under the Defense Acquisition University).

- The Defense Acquisition University has revised three courses from the Basic Contracting Curriculum to address pricing issues. These updated courses have been offered since autumn 1999. Information about Defense Acquisition University courses can be found at http://www.dau.mil.

> *Basics of Contracting* (CON 101) is a survey course encompassing the entire contracting process from the receipt of a purchase request through contract completion, including closeout, with emphasis on commercial contracting. The updated course includes two hours of discussion on price analysis and cost analysis techniques.

> *Principles of Contract Pricing* (CON 104) provides essential fundamentals for the study and practice of price, cost, and proposal analysis. It also provides a discussion and demonstration of applicable estimating techniques used to support these analyses. Topics include a review of the contracting environment, the use and importance of market research, sources of data for price or cost analysis, and the application of price-related factors in determining reasonableness.

> The terminal objective of *Intermediate Contract Pricing* (CON 204) is for students to recognize pricing issues and develop prenegotiation objectives so that a fair and reasonable price position is supported in contract actions. One of the primary course objectives is for students to understand how to use market research and the contracting officer's commerciality decision to determine the required price or cost data.

◆ The National Association of Purchasing Managers and the National Contract Management Association teamed to offer online courses. Their Web-based course *Integrating Commercial Practices with Government Business Practices, Program I: Managing Suppliers* (#3900) can be found at http://www.napm-ncma.org. This course includes three learning modules: (1) Concepts of Integrating Commercial Practices, (2) Managing Suppliers and Commercial Practices, and (3) Improving Supply Chain Performance. In the second module, price and cost analyses are discussed as tools that help in the selection of good suppliers. Factors that affect supplier prices are covered in detail, with special recognition given to the need for analyzing prices that reflect commercial, market-driven, supply-demand situations, including prices affected by Government-unique requirements. The course has been available since February 1999. More than 4,000 Defense personnel have taken it.

◆ The Defense Acquisition University, the Department of the Army, and the University of Virginia's Darden Graduate School of Business partnered to develop the course *Competing in a New Business Environment: A Program for Defense Acquisition Executives*. This course was developed specifically to address the perceived deficiency in the knowledge of Government personnel about what drives private-sector business decisions. This course is held biannually, offering students exposure to real business case studies, guest corporate and Government lecturers, and a follow-up session identifying lessons learned for implementation by the Department. Dr. Bob Ainsley (703-805-4565) is the DAU point of contact for this course; for information regarding specifics on course content, he can be contacted at bob.ainsley@dau.mil.

◆ The Defense Contract Management Agency and the Defense Contract Audit Agency chartered the Joint Industry/Government Parametric Cost Estimating Initiative. This group—including members from both of the chartering organizations, the military services, and representatives of industry—prepared a *Parametric Cost Estimating Handbook*. Parametric estimating is an acceptable method, according to the Federal Acquisition Regulation, for preparing proposals based on cost or pricing data or other types of data. This handbook is a guide for industry and Government acquisition professionals who prepare, evaluate, or negotiate proposals by using parametric estimating techniques. The *Parametric Cost Estimating Handbook* can be found at http://www.ispa-cost.org/PEIWeb/cover.htm.

◆ The Defense Acquisition University offers, in addition to the three basic courses described above, *Advanced Contract Pricing* (CON 235). This course is designed for buyers, price analysts, and contracting officers tasked with obtaining fair and reasonable prices in today's Defense acquisition environment. The course addresses understanding market forces and the market research process critical to deciding whether an acquisition should be commercial. The course explores the application of quantitative tools used in price analysis for commercial items and price or cost analysis for noncommercial items. Statistical analyses and parametric methods are examined. The following topics are covered during course discussions, exercises, and cases within the course: Market Research, Developing an Estimating Tool, Analogy Technique, Parametric Estimating, Computer Software Applications, Best Value, Integrated Product Team Pricing, Getting Expert Opinions, and Commercial Item Pricing. Information about this and other Defense Acquisition University courses can be found at http://www.dau.mil.

◆ Air Force Materiel Command's (AFMC's) Directorate of Contracting (Pricing, Finance and Specialized Policy [PKPC]) has developed and made available the student workbook from the two-hour *Commercial Item Pricing* training and *Price-Based Acquisition* training. Additionally, a briefing given by Headquarters AFMC/PKPC on *Commercial Item Pricing* specifically addresses lessons learned during an actual case study. These and other Air Force market research and pricing tools can be found at http://www.safaq.hq.af.mil/contracting/toolkit/.

◆ The Assistant Secretary of the Navy (Research, Development and Acquisition) issued a June 1997 memorandum highlighting problems experienced in pricing commercial items. This policy memorandum informs the acquisition community that some sole-source firms are proposing commercial items at catalog prices that reflect excessive increases over the prices charged when the same items were previously bought using cost or pricing data. This memorandum instructs contracting officers to understand the basis of catalog prices and encourages the use of market research, and it provides guidance about the types of information that can be used to determine price reasonableness. The memorandum can be found at http://www.abm.rda.hq.navy.mil/abm97_11.html.

◆ The Office of the Director, Defense Acquisition Initiatives also offers the Commercial Advocates Forum Web site. This site promotes the acquisition of commercial items and the use of commercial practices by disseminating information to front-line buyers, enabling the exchange of questions and answers, and sharing best practices and lessons learned. By visiting the Commercial Advocates Forum as part of the market research effort, acquisition personnel can make contacts for similar acquisitions. The Forum offers extensive data focused on commercial item acquisition, including news and success stories, links to agency commercial advocates, and a library of resources and tools that can help to simplify the market research effort. As has been previously stated, market research is a key method for determining whether a proposed price is fair and reasonable, and data from buyers and other experts are important to consider as part of your market research. The Commercial Advocates Forum Web site can be found at http://www.cadv.org.

◆ The Commercial Advocates Forum offers access to the General Accounting Office report *DoD Pricing of Commercial Items Needs Continued Emphasis* at http://www.cadv.org/pdf_docs/mrhandbook.pdf.

Appendix R
Mandatory Commercial Item Terms and Conditions

COMMERCIAL ITEM TERMS AND CONDITIONS

The solicitation and the subsequent contract are transformed under commercial item acquisitions. Both have fewer solicitation provisions and contract clauses than solicitations and contracts generated under acquisitions using Government-unique policies and procedures. By statute, contracts acquiring commercial items, to the maximum extent practicable, can include only those contract clauses that

- are required to implement law or Executive Order, or

- are determined to be consistent with "standard commercial practice."

  "Standard commercial practice" refers to the customs of companies in a particular marketplace, regardless of the practices of an individual firm in that marketplace (e.g., a term may be standard in the marketplace even if a firm does not normally use that specific term in its own practices).

  To implement this mandate, the Federal Acquisition Regulation (FAR) has limited solicitation provisions and contract clauses specifically developed for commercial items. Notwithstanding the prescriptions for provisions and clauses contained throughout the rest of the FAR, the only provisions and clauses the contracting officer is *required* to use are those which are prescribed in FAR Part 12. This fact greatly eases the process of preparing solicitations and contracts for commercial items, and it should prevent provisions and clauses not appropriate for commercial items from creeping into these acquisitions. The contracting officer does have the flexibility to use other provisions and clauses, including FAR provisions and clauses, but only when

- their use is consistent with customary commercial practices, and

- the contractor agrees to their use, or

- a waiver to use terms and conditions inconsistent with customary commercial practice is obtained in accordance with agency procedures.

  In acquiring commercial items, agencies can supplement the FAR Part 12 provisions and clauses, but only if

- necessary to reflect agency-unique statutes, or

- approved by the agency senior procurement executive or the agency's representative to the FAR Council (this approval authority cannot be delegated).

Tailoring Provisions and Clauses

The contracting officer can tailor the commercial item provisions and clauses to adapt to the particular commercial market in which he or she is working. The basic terms and conditions prescribed in the Part 12 provisions and clauses strike a balance between the interests of both the buyer and the seller, the unique requirements of Federal Government acquisitions, and the common desire for brevity and clarity. These provisions and clauses, however, may not be appropriate for all transactions. Thus, the FAR recognizes that the contracting officer is in the best position on a given acquisition to evaluate the market situation, assess the Government's position in the market for that item, and appropriately tailor the terms and conditions to that situation. But, while the FAR gives contracting officers broad authority to tailor solicitations and contracts where the tailoring is consistent with commercial practices, any tailoring in a manner inconsistent with commercial practice must be approved in accordance with agency procedures.

The solicitation provision at FAR 52.212-3 may be tailored, but only in accordance with FAR Subpart 1.4, Deviations from the FAR. Tailoring can be accomplished by including other provisions or clauses from the FAR, a FAR supplement, or a commercial source, in whole in part, or by drafting new language to provide necessary coverage on topics not addressed in the FAR Part 12 provisions and clauses.

The provisions at FAR 52.212-1 and 52.212-2 and the clause at 52.212-4 can be tailored. However, certain specified paragraphs of the clause at FAR 52.212-4 implement statutory requirements and cannot be tailored (see FAR 12.302[b]).

To promote efficiency and economy under the FAR 13.5 Simplified Acquisition Procedures Test Program, tailoring may be applied to a range of items provided by the contractor rather than to individual item acquisitions.

The clause at 52.212-5, Contract Terms and Conditions Required to Implement Statutes or Executive Orders—Commercial Items, incorporates by reference only those clauses required to implement provisions of law or Executive Orders applicable to the acquisition of commercial items. The clause at 52.212-5, Contract Terms and Conditions, is not required for COTS items, which have their own alternative Contract Terms and Conditions clause. Neither clause may be tailored (but see the following paragraph).

Certain revisions to the FAR Part 12 provisions and clauses are *not* considered tailoring. For example, when fast payment procedures are authorized, contracting officers may revise paragraph (i) of the clause at FAR 52.212-4 accordingly. Also, contracting officers may delete from solicitations and contracts portions of the provision at FAR 52.212-3 and the clause at FAR 52.212-5 that do not apply and replace them with applicable language, if any (e.g., when guidance for DoD differs from that in the FAR, when a deviation applies, or when only supplies are being acquired and requirements related solely to services can be omitted).

Contract Clauses

Contracts for acquiring commercial items include, to the maximum extent practicable, only those clauses required to implement provisions of law or Executive Orders applicable to the acquisition of commercial items or determined to be consistent with customary commercial practice. The clauses at FAR 52.212-4 and 52.212-5 either embody those clauses or incorporate them by reference. The contracting officer is responsible for reviewing these clauses to thoroughly understand their applicability.

Within the clause at FAR 52.212-5, the clauses cited in its paragraph (a) are automatically applicable, whereas those listed in paragraph (b) are applicable only when the contracting officer checks them as appropriate for the circumstances. The automatically applicable clauses are those at FAR 52.222-3, Convict Labor, and 52.233-3, Protest after Award; they cannot be tailored. However, they might be self-deleting in certain circumstances. For example, the Convict Labor clause is self-deleting for most contracts performed overseas because it applies only to circumstances where convict labor is available from any state, the District of Columbia, the Commonwealth of Puerto Rico, the Virgin Islands, Guam, American Samoa, the Commonwealth of the Northern Mariana Islands, or the Trust Territory of the Pacific Islands (FAR 22.202). However, addenda to the solicitation and contract should *not* be used to indicate that a clause listed in FAR 52.212-5 (a) is self-deleting, since addenda are the specific means for tailoring a provision or clause, and the clause at FAR 52.212-5 cannot be tailored, as noted previously.

SUBCONTRACTING FOR COMMERCIAL ITEMS

The Federal Acquisition Streamlining Act of 1994 (FASA) encourages, to the maximum extent practicable, the acquisition of commercial items at the subcontractor level. To extend the benefits of commercial item acquisitions to the subcontractor level, Government contracts contain limitations on the applicability of certain laws to the acquisition of commercial items at the subcontractor level, including a transfer of commercial items between divisions, subsidiaries, or affiliates of a contractor or subcontractor. This flow-down limitation is addressed in two ways:

- ◆ The clause at 52.212-5, Contract Terms and Conditions Required to Implement Statutes or Executive Orders—Commercial Items which goes in all prime contracts *for commercial items*, contains a paragraph (e) that limits the required flow-down of clauses to subcontractors to just four FAR clauses.

- ◆ The clause at FAR 52.244-6, Subcontracts for Commercial Items and Commercial Components, which goes in all prime *contracts for other than commercial items*, states that, notwithstanding any other clause in the contract, the contractor is not required to include any FAR provision or clause other than those listed in this clause.

These clauses offer significant incentives to encourage the expanded use of commercial items at all tiers. Either of these clauses is the only *required* clause for prime contractors to flow down to subcontracts, but the prime contractor can flow down other provisions and clauses, including FAR provisions and clauses, as necessary to meet its obligations under the prime contract.

Appendix S
Buying Commercial Items through Multiple-Award Task and Delivery Order Contracts and Multiple-Award Schedules

Multiple-award task and delivery-order contracts and the multiple award schedules (MAS) have become increasingly popular procurement vehicles for satisfying agency needs. These vehicles were designed as a means for efficiently applying competitive pressures to a small number of capable contractors before placing orders. If used effectively, these vehicles can facilitate the timely acquisition of commercial items and the latest innovations offered in the marketplace.

MULTIPLE-AWARD TASK AND DELIVERY ORDER CONTRACTS

The Federal Acquisition Streamlining Act of 1994 (FASA) clarified agencies' authority to award multiple task and delivery order contracts covering the same scope of services or products and to award orders for specific work after giving each contract holder a fair opportunity to be considered. The streamlined, commercial-style competition offers customers the opportunity to take advantage of advances in technology and changes in agency priorities in a timely manner.

A variety of agencies have made their multiple-award task and delivery order contracts available for ordering by other agencies, especially those offering information technology (IT) products and services. Interagency multiple-award task and delivery order contracts for IT are referred to either as Government-wide acquisition contracts (GWACs) or multi-agency contracts. GWACs are structured for use by agencies Government-wide and are operated by designated executive agents. Multi-agency contracts may, but need not, be structured to support Government-wide use and are operated by agencies pursuant to the Economy Act. Also, the scope of a multi-agency contract need not be limited to IT.

MULTIPLE-AWARD SCHEDULES

The MAS are a listing of multiple contractors, each of which has been awarded a contract by the General Services Administration (GSA) (or by the Department of Veterans Affairs [VA] for pharmaceuticals and other medical supplies) for use by all Federal agencies. The MAS are structured to provide buyer access to a wide range of commonly used commercial supplies and services through a large cadre of qualified suppliers so that agencies have considerable flexibility in fulfilling their broad-ranging requirements. Processes for using the MAS are highly streamlined and simplified. Access to additional information, ordering, and payment is facilitated through the Web site of the Federal Supply Schedules (http://www.fss.gsa.gov/schedules/) and GSA Advantage!,™ an electronic catalog of the items in the GSA supply system. When acquiring services through the schedules, refer to GSA's "special ordering procedures," available at http://www.fss.gsa.gov/schedules/ordinssv.cfm.

KEY CONSIDERATIONS

1. *What should an agency consider in deciding when an existing multiple-award task and delivery order contract (or GWAC or multi-agency contract) or MAS will serve as an effective means for satisfying its needs for commercial items?*

In conducting market research and acquisition planning, agencies should consider the potentially beneficial terms and conditions and competitive pricing (as well as administrative savings) of multiple-award task and delivery order contracts and MAS. In doing so, agencies are responsible for determining, as they identify and gain an understanding of marketplace capabilities, whether the focus and terms and conditions of an existing contract will result in an optimal fit between agency needs and commercial solutions. The MAS program, for example, offers an array of commonly used commercial products and services. Use of the MAS, therefore, may be less effective when more tailored commercial solutions better suit the agency requirement. A multiple-award task and delivery order contract provides the opportunity to encourage a set of contractors to compete for buys in a particular category or by a particular set of users. If a customer is likely to have significant recurring needs for supplies or services that fall within the scope of existing multiple-award task and delivery order contracts, but are not the main focus of those contracts, the customer may be able to achieve better prices and terms and conditions by establishing a new task and delivery order contract or other appropriate contract type.

The successful use of multiple-award task and delivery order contracts and MAS, like the successful use of any other acquisition tool, requires the commitment and cooperation of all agency disciplines responsible for the agency's mission. Thus, it is important to secure the cross-functional cooperation of contracting, program, finance, and legal offices in taking responsibility for the effective planning and execution of orders using these vehicles.

2. *What should an agency consider in setting up a multiple-award task and delivery order contract?*[2]

Multiple-award task and delivery order contracts are effective only when they are structured, managed, and administered to consistently take full advantage of the fair opportunity process. While awardees need not be equally capable in all areas, contracting officers need to avoid situations in which awardees specialize exclusively in one or a few areas within the statement of work, since this practice will increase the likelihood that orders in these areas will be awarded on a sole-source basis.

The presence of multiple qualified sources to which the Government has efficient access is key to sustaining access to the competitive pressures of the marketplace. In determining the number

---

[2] GSA (and VA through a delegation from GSA for certain medical products) is statutorily responsible for establishing schedules for Government-wide use. The creation of new schedules is based on, among other things, the level of demand for a product or service line.

of contracts to be awarded under a multiple-award task and delivery order contract, the contracting officer should consider (1) the scope and complexity of the contract requirement, (2) the expected duration and frequency of task or delivery orders, (3) the mix of resources a contractor possesses to meet the expected task or delivery order requirements, and (4) the ability to maintain competition among the awardees throughout the contracts' periods of performance.

The initial contract should include provisions that reflect the Government's buying power (e.g., caps on prices for defined tasks, and capped hourly rates). If a multiple-award task and delivery order contract is to provide access to products or services that fall both within and outside Part 12, the contract must include the Part 12 clauses for commercial buys.

3. *How can an agency take full advantage of the benefits offered by established multiple-award task and delivery order contracts and MAS in buying commercial items?*

The potential of multiple-award task and delivery order contracts and MAS to deliver good overall deals for the taxpayer too often goes unrealized. Optimizing results on multiple-award task and delivery order contracts and MAS requires that (1) orders be effectively structured, (2) competitive pressures be applied in order placement, and (3) the division of responsibilities between the servicing agency and the customer be well understood.

STRUCTURING ORDERS

Customers of multiple-award task and delivery order contracts and MAS should structure orders to facilitate effective mission attainment. In particular, they should do the following:

♦ **Make task orders for services performance-based.** As generally is the case when describing agency needs (see Chapter 1), customers are responsible for focusing on desired mission-related outcomes instead of emphasizing how the work is to be performed, and tie payment to the contractor's successes in achieving those outcomes. Doing so will motivate improved performance and reduce contract prices.

♦ **Think modular.** Multiple-award task and delivery order contracts and MAS are well suited to help customers manage risk. By providing ready access to a cadre of qualified contractors, these vehicles enable customers to pursue projects in manageable segments (typically narrow in scope and brief in duration) that can independently deliver mission benefits with the confidence that additional segments may be acquired in a timely fashion. If a longer-term order is appropriate, the customer should incorporate effective "off ramps" to minimize dependence on one contractor. Unnecessarily large and inadequately defined orders will make it difficult to apply competitive pressures and need to be avoided.

ORDER PLACEMENT

To make the most of multiple-award task and delivery order contracts and MAS, it is imperative for customers to capitalize on the competition made possible under these contracts and to take price into consideration before placing an order.

TAKING ADVANTAGE OF COMPETITIVE PRESSURES

Multiple-Award Contracts

Multiple-award task and delivery order contracts generate sustained competitive pressure within the vehicle through a process whereby contract holders are given a fair opportunity to be considered for specific requirements through streamlined ordering procedures. Thus, to reap these benefits of these contracts, customers are responsible for doing the following:

♦ **Providing each awardee a fair opportunity to be considered for each order (over $2,500).** Methods that would not result in giving fair consideration to each awardee, such as allocation or designation of a preferred awardee, must not be used. Four exceptions to the fair opportunity process are recognized in law and regulation. If the ordering office intends to use an exception to the fair opportunity process, it might consider announcing this intention. Another contract holder may express an interest that may prove worthy of consideration.

Submission requirements should be kept to a minimum, with emphasis on streamlined procedures, such as oral presentations. For product buys, it may be unnecessary to require each awardee to develop a separate proposal, and it may be unnecessary to conduct negotiations with each awardee prior to awarding a delivery order. A streamlined approach is warranted if the contracting officer or customer can compare the various prices and products being offered under these contracts, consider each awardee, and make an award in the best interest of the Government.

It is important that ordering decisions be properly and adequately documented. The contracting officer is responsible for documenting in the contract file the rationale for placement and price of each order, including the basis for award and the rationale for any tradeoffs among cost or price and non-cost considerations in making the award decision. This documentation need not quantify the tradeoffs that led to the decision. The contract file needs to identify the basis for using an exception to the fair opportunity process. If the agency uses the logical follow-on exception, it is important that the rationale describe why the relationship between the initial order and the follow-on is logical (e.g., in terms of scope, period of performance, or value).

♦ **Fostering effective communication.** Effective communication between Government customers and contract holders is essential for ensuring the routine receipt of more than one viable business solution and for maximizing situations where the customer is choosing between competing offers. This communication is especially important where the ordering office lacks information to define a solution in performance-based terms and proposal development is resource-intensive. In acquiring systems and services in particular, dialogue will typically be necessary to ensure that requirements and risks are well understood. This understanding is needed so that contract holders can develop and propose realistic, well-defined solutions that best match Government needs with commercially available marketplace capabilities and enable the Government to award performance-based orders.

Accordingly, customers should take steps to ensure that contract holders are able to make effective business decisions in deciding whether and how to propose. Among other things, sufficient time should be provided for contract holders to review requirements for orders. In addition, techniques should be considered that facilitate effective information exchange and contractor investigation, such as through the distribution of draft statements of work.

Multiple-Award Schedules

The MAS, with its wide range of products and services and its large cadre of qualified contractors, provides customers with broad access to the commercial marketplace for commonly used commercial items. As is the case with ordering under multiple-award task and delivery order contracts, the effective use of competitive pressures, including good communications with contractors, and the appropriate documentation of activities, are important for MAS purchases. While the fair opportunity process applicable to multiple-award task and delivery order contracts does not apply to MAS ordering, FAR Subpart 8.4 envisions the application of competitive pressures through the consideration of multiple MAS contractors on orders above $2,500.

Supplies. For orders for supplies over $2,500 up to the maximum order (MO) threshold, agencies are expected to review information through GSA Advantage!^{TM} or price lists/catalogs of at least three schedule contractors.

Services. For services, GSA's special ordering procedures require customers to request quotations from three schedule contractors if the order is over $2,500 and under the MO threshold. The procedures envision customers preparing performance-based statements of work and placing firm-fixed-price orders based on the prices in the schedule and with consideration of the mix of labor categories and level of effort required to perform the services described in the statement of work. The customer is required to make a determination that the total price of a particular order is fair and reasonable.

The MO threshold is included to serve as a marker above which customers need to consider additional contractors (beyond the three otherwise considered) and generally seek price reductions.

Pursuant to Federal Acquisition Regulation (FAR) 8.404(b)(4), customers should consider setting up single or multiple blanket purchase agreements (BPAs) with schedule contractors to satisfy recurring needs. BPAs are designed to further reduce the administrative burden associated with order placement and invoicing while permitting agencies to secure additional discounts for repetitive or higher volume purchasing.

CONSIDERING PRICE

In order to obtain best value, orders need to take price into consideration. It is important that individual orders clearly describe all services to be performed or supplies to be delivered so the full cost or price for performance of the work can be established when the order is placed. Orders must be priced consistent with FAR Part 12 guidance on contract types. Fixed prices will provide an incentive for contractors to control costs and perform efficiently.

GSA negotiates prices for the MAS. Per FAR 8.404(a), agencies may rely on GSA prices as fair and reasonable. However, as noted above, if a purchase is likely to exceed the MO threshold, agencies are expected to generally ask for better pricing. According to GSA's special ordering procedures, available at http://www/fss.gsa.gov/schedules/, applicable to the acquisition of services, the ordering office is expected to determine that the total firm fixed price it negotiates—after considering rates identified in the GSA schedules—is fair and reasonable.

Considerations other than price also play an important role. Considering past performance in the comparative evaluation of contract holders will enable agencies to better predict the quality of, and customer satisfaction with, future work and is instrumental in making best-value selections. Moreover, evaluating proposals that contain different technical approaches will likely require tradeoffs between solutions and different risks and benefits. Customers are expected to use good business judgment to determine appropriate methods for considering risk management, cost control, quality differences, and other considerations relevant to order placement. And, as noted above, adequately documenting ordering decisions is important.

UNDERSTANDING RESPONSIBILITIES

Because acquisitions under MAS and many acquisitions under multiple-award task and delivery order contracts are inter-agency, it is important that customers clearly understand what they are expected to do (especially since the division of responsibilities may vary between vehicles). For example, there should be a clear understanding of who is responsible for program quality and control to measure contract performance and ensure successful completion of tasks.

When engaging in interagency acquisitions, even when the Economy Act does not apply (such as to MAS and GWACs), customers still must comply with the FAR and applicable statutes, Executive Orders, and guidance (e.g., relevant to acquisition planning, development of an information technology strategy, and obligation of appropriations) (see 31 U.S.C. 1501(a)(1)). In addition, DoD customers are required (pursuant to 10 U.S.C. 2225(b)(5)(B)) to identify the reasons for making a purchase through an agency other than the Department of Defense.

www.ingramcontent.com/pod-product-compliance
Lightning Source LLC
Chambersburg PA
CBHW082143290526
45794CB00008B/3147